Science and Literature
A conference

Science and Literature
A conference

Library of Congress · Washington · 1985

ACKNOWLEDGMENTS

"Loneliness" from *95 poems* by e. e. cummings, copyright 1958 by Harcourt, Brace & Company. Reprinted by permission of Harcourt Brace Jovanovich, Inc.

"Avenidas" and "Silencio" by Eugen Gomringer, "Beba" by Décio Pignatari, "Schützengraben" by Ernst Jandl, "Magic of a Summer Night" by Ladislav Novák, "The Echo of the Gold," by Mathias Goeritz, "du/dich/ich" by Oswald Wiener, and "Moonshot Sonnet" by Mary Ellen Solt from *Concrete Poetry: A World View*, edited by Mary Ellen Solt, copyright 1969 by Indiana University Press. Reprinted by permission of Indiana University Press.

"Tributes to Henry Ford" by Richard Kostelanetz from *Visual Language*, copyright 1970 by Assembling Press. Reprinted by permission of Assembling Press.

"The Computer's First Christmas Card" by Edwin Morgan from *Poems of Thirty Years* (Manchester, England), copyright 1982 by Edwin Morgan. Reprinted by permission of Carcanet Press Limited.

Library of Congress Cataloging in Publication Data
Main entry under title:

Science and literature.

   Papers and discussions from the Conference on Science and Literature, Nov. 9-10, 1981, held at the Library of Congress.
   1. Literature and science—Congresses. I. Conference on Science and Literature (1981: Library of Congress)
PN55.S36   1985   809'.9355   84-20121
ISBN 0-8444-0477-2

Available from the Library of Congress, Central Services Division, Washington, D.C. 20540

THE GERTRUDE CLARKE WHITTALL POETRY AND LITERATURE FUND

The Gertrude Clarke Whittall Poetry and Literature Fund was established in the Library of Congress in December 1950, through the generosity of Mrs. Gertrude Clarke Whittall, in order to create a center in this country for the development and encouragement of poetry, drama, and literature. Mrs. Whittall's earlier benefactions include the presentation to the Library of a number of important literary manuscripts, a gift of five magnificent Stradivari instruments, the endowment of an annual series of concerts of chamber music, and the formation of a collection of music manuscripts that has no parallel in the Western Hemisphere.

The Poetry and Literature Fund allows the Library to offer poetry readings, lectures, and dramatic performances. The proceedings of this conference are published by the Library to reach a wider audience and as a contribution to literary history and criticism.

CONTENTS

Preface   ix
Participants   xi

SESSION 1   November 9, 1981

Welcoming Remarks   3
   DANIEL J. BOORSTIN, *The Librarian of Congress*
Science and the World Beyond   3
   GEORGE WALD, *Higgins Professor of Biology, emeritus, Harvard University*
Discussion   22
   MAXINE KUMIN, *Moderator, Consultant in Poetry, Library of Congress, 1981–82*

SESSION 2   November 10, 1981

The Poetry of Nothing   41
   O. B. HARDISON, *Director, Folger Shakespeare Library, 1969–84*
Discussion   53
   WILLIAM MEREDITH, *Moderator, Consultant in Poetry, Library of Congress, 1978–80*

SESSION 3   November 10, 1981

The Outlook for Science and Literature: Open Discussion   85
   JAMES BEALL, *Moderator, National Academy of Sciences / National Research Council, Research Associate, Naval Research Laboratory*

APPENDIX:

The Poetry of Nothing   135
   O. B. HARDISON

PREFACE

The idea for a conference on science and literature originated with the late Robert Hayden during his term as consultant in poetry to the Library of Congress, 1976–78. Mr. Hayden was especially interested in the literature of science fantasy. At that time some overtures were made to five persons thought to be essential to such a conference. Unfortunately, the majority of those approached were unavailable at a time convenient to the Library. Mr. Hayden and I then agreed to defer such a conference.

When William Meredith, Mr. Hayden's successor, became consultant in poetry, I acquainted him with discussions and abortive actions concerning such a conference. At first unenthusiastic, Mr. Meredith became increasingly intrigued with the possibilities of such a conference. With the assistance of a local scientist/poet, James Beall, Mr. Meredith arranged three gatherings of Washington-area scientists and writers to define some issues and find some common ground for discussion by a larger and more diversified group. From those preliminary meetings derived the Library of Congress conference reported in this volume. By the time a full-scale conference could be planned, Mr. Meredith's term as consultant had also expired. Although the conference took place during the term of his successor, Maxine Kumin, Mr. Meredith was able to return to Washington for the occasion and to play a significant role in the planning and the success of the event. Thus, three successive consultants in poetry contributed to the Conference on Science and Literature in November 1981.

There have been numerous conferences on various aspects of literature sponsored by the Library of Congress, through its Gertrude Clarke Whittall Poetry and Literature Fund or with the assistance of outside foundations and organizations. The most memorable, no doubt, was the three-day National Poetry Festival in October 1962, which coincided, by chance, with the Cuban Missile Crisis. Historians of the future may find it instructive to ponder the ironies inherent in a gathering of some of the country's leading poets and critics for three days of readings, lectures, and literary discussions while the nation came close to East/West confrontation.

In conferences preceding that on science and literature—including the National Poetry Festival—there have been "participants" and "audience." For the Conference on Science and Literature, it was decided to break that pattern. Only one open public event was scheduled, an evening of readings by Diane Ackerman, Philip Appleman, John Gardner, Ursula Le Guin, and Gene Roddenberry. The remainder of the conference was by invitation only. Some forty persons came together for three sessions of discussion, which was prompted by two papers, one by Nobel laureate George Wald and one by Folger Shakespeare Library director O. B. Hardison. But the papers were mere springboards for wide-ranging reactions and counterreactions, some far removed from the topics introduced by the papers.

Thus did the Conference on Science and Literature take on a life of its own and become a true *conference*. It moved in its own directions, unmindful of the efforts of its moderators to contain it. It was, at times, decidedly immoderate. Participants became peeved or disgusted, and one withdrew himself, only to return to the circle of discussion later. There were disagreements, changing alliances, and obscure harmonies in the dynamics of the two-day meeting. At the end there were no pronouncements, as in diplomatic summits, but there was a sense of resolution and coherence, which each participant would undoubtedly express in his or her own way, in his or her own poetic or scientific vocabulary.

The record of the conference is offered, therefore, not as "proceedings" but as the retrospective scenario of a memorable gathering in the Library of Congress, in which partisans of different perspectives and ways of viewing human existence shouted at, insulted, disagreed with, but ultimately *listened* to each other.

John C. Broderick
Assistant Librarian for Research Services

PARTICIPANTS

DIANE ACKERMAN
Department of English, University of Pittsburgh
KARREN ALENIER
Author, Chevy Chase, Maryland
PHILIP APPLEMAN
Departments of English, Columbia and Indiana Universities
STEPHEN S. BARATZ
Clinical Psychologist, Washington, D.C.
JAMES BEALL
National Academy of Science, Washington, D.C.
WENDELL BERRY
Author, Port Royal, Kentucky
DANIEL J. BOORSTIN
The Librarian of Congress
RUTH F. BOORSTIN
Writer, Washington, D.C.
JOHN C. BRODERICK
Assistant Librarian for Research Services, Library of Congress
GAIL FINSTERBUSCH
Sociologist, Washington, D.C.
NANCY GALBRAITH
Special Assistant in Poetry, Library of Congress
JOHN GARDNER
Department of English, General Literature and Rhetoric, State University of New York at Binghamton
PATRICIA GARFINKEL
Author, Reston, Virginia
MICHAEL GLASER
English Department, St. Mary's College (Maryland)
RICHARD GROSSMAN
Environmentalists for Full Employment, Washington, D.C.
O. B. HARDISON
Director, Folger Shakespeare Library, 1969–84
SIR FRED HOYLE
Royal Society, London, England
ANN KELLY
English Department, Howard University
HENRY KELLY
Physicist, Washington, D.C.
MAXINE KUMIN
Consultant in Poetry, Library of Congress, 1981–82
VICTOR M. KUMIN
Engineer, Warner, New Hampshire
PRAMOD LAD
Kaiser Research Laboratory, Los Angeles, California

ALLAN LEFCOWITZ
Director, Writers Center, Washington, D.C.
MERRILL LEFFLER
English Department, U.S. Naval Academy
PAUL DONALD MACLEAN
Laboratory of Brain Evolution and Behavior, National Institute of Mental Health
GAIL H. MARCUS
Assistant Chief, Science Policy Research Division, Library of Congress
CAROLINE MARSHALL
Author, Washington, D.C.
WILLIAM MATHESON
Chief, Rare Book and Special Collections Division, Library of Congress
WILLIAM MEREDITH
English Department, Connecticut College; Consultant in Poetry, Library of Congress, 1978–80
ROBERTA BALSTAD MILLER
Social Science Research Council, Washington, D.C.

Conference participants Gene Roddenberry, Robert Sokolowski, Richard Seltzer, and Robert Sargent

Conference participants Merrill Leffler, Diane Ackerman, and Philip Appleman

WALTER JAMES MILLER
    English Department, New York University
LINDA PASTAN
    Author, Potomac, Maryland
JERRY POURNELLE
    Author, Studio City, California
JOSEPH PRICE
    Chief, Science and Technology Division, Library of Congress
GENE RODDENBERRY
    Author, Beverly Hills, California
ROBERT SARGENT
    Author, Arlington, Virginia
RICHARD WARREN SELTZER, JR.
    Author, West Roxbury, Massachusetts
MYRA SKLAREW
    Department of Literature, American University
ROBERT SOKOLOWSKI
    School of Philosophy, Catholic University of America
GEORGE WALD
    Biochemist, Cambridge, Massachusetts

The conference allowed for informal as well as formal discussions among the participants—such as this conversation between Wendell Berry and Karren Alenier during a break for coffee.

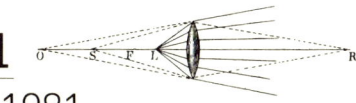

SESSION 1
November 9, 1981

Welcoming Remarks
DANIEL J. BOORSTIN

Science and the World Beyond
GEORGE WALD

Discussion
MAXINE KUMIN, Moderator

Librarian of Congress Daniel J. Boorstin addresses the opening session of the conference in the Library's Wilson Room. **Conference participants seated around the table, left to right:** Patricia Garfinkel, O. B. Hardison, Wendell Berry (partially hidden), Allan Lefcowitz, Jerry Pournelle, Myra Sklarew, Linda Pastan, Philip Appleman, Diane Ackerman, James Beall, Victor Kumin, Merrill Leffler, William Matheson, Ruth Boorstin, William Meredith, Maxine Kumin, George Wald, Daniel Boorstin

DANIEL J. BOORSTIN: We are pleased that you are all here today, and we are indebted to the Poetry Office, and especially to Maxine, for arranging it. I do want to welcome you here. I hope that for those of you for whom this is the first time in the Library, you'll consider this to be an introduction to the Library of Congress, that you'll come back again and again to your library. I will simply say that the subject of this conference today, science and literature, is about as good a three-word summary of the problems of the Library of Congress as you could find. In a cliché which I am sure you all will recall, Ezra Pound once said that literature is news which stays news. But we might almost say that science is news which becomes obsolete, or which we hope will become obsolete with tomorrow's news. Science is the realm of the up-to-date, the latest word, and literature is the accumulated tradition and wisdom which becomes richer with the patina of the past. So it is especially appropriate that you should be considering this if you will imagine the difference between the problem of building a scientific library, which could be very small, since you'd only have the most recent information in it, with that of building a great library of literature, which the Library of Congress is, and which must have works in all languages from all ages, in which we do not take upon us the arrogance of arbitrating obsolescence. You will see the significance of this conference and the point at which we are meeting.

I am especially pleased to be here with Professor Wald, a former teacher of mine, and I look forward to hearing what he has to tell us.

GEORGE WALD: (changing his position) I'll join the poets.

Since Mr. Broderick was so kind as to ask me to this meeting, thoughts have been flooding upon me in such profusion that I will just find my way through this talk, hoping to stop reasonably soon so the discussion I most look forward to can take place.

What most divides men from the beasts is the capacity to know and to create: *homo sapiens et faber*. The knowing is epitomized in science, the creating in the arts. And, in fact, this state of things is projected upon the human brain. As the great neurosurgeon Wilder Penfield showed years ago, there lies along that deep groove, the central sulcus of the cerebrum, on one side a projection of sensory man and on the other side a projection of motor man. Each of them is laid out pretty well in the pattern of the body, so that one has two little men in the brain, two *homunculi,* a sensory and a motor. If one makes a picture of this projection, of those two *homunculi,* one sees an extraordinary distortion: enormous hands and an enormous mouth. Man is the talking and the handling animal; and his talking and handling have much to do with his making and knowing.

Of course, science and the arts—and for us here science and literature—should not be, and until relatively recently were not, as separate as they are now. There have been numerous cross-currents: authors talking science, even mathematics ("Euclid alone has looked on Beauty bare!" Millay); and scientists expressing in their science an awe and ecstasy that make of it high literature. The examples come in profusion; let me just offer you two: a scientist making literature and an author making use of mathematical physics.

The scientist I want to cite is Isaac Newton. There never has been another scientist like Newton. Since I have spent most of my life teaching in the university, I realize that his life contains a lesson for us that we teachers haven't considered. What happened to Newton was that he went to Cambridge University, to Trinity College—one is still shown the windows of his room, over the entrance. Then, after he had learned a few things—some science, some mathematics—the plague came, and he went home to Woolthorpe, his village, to rusticate for two years. During two years that probably bored him enormously, he became intimate with the universe; so that by the end of that time he seemed to know intuitively what kinds of things to expect of it and what to exclude.

An example: you've all heard the story of the falling apple, which may be apocryphal; but I'll tell you another that's not apocryphal.

The forces that govern the planetary motions had been a matter of intense discussion in the Royal Society of London. Early in 1684 its secretary, Robert Hooke, in a conversation with Sir Christopher Wren (an artist?—the architect of St. Paul's!) and the astronomer Edmund Halley (the comet!), claimed to have demonstrated that the orbits of the planets follow from an inverse square law of gravitation. Wren said that if Hooke would provide a proof of that within two months, he would give Hooke a book worth forty shillings. Hooke never came through with the proof. In August 1684, Halley went down to Cambridge and asked Newton what would be the shape of the orbit of a planet attracted to the sun by a gravitational force varying as the square of the distance. Newton immediately replied, an ellipse. "Struck with joy and amazement," Halley asked how Newton knew that. Newton said that he had calculated it; but on being urged couldn't lay hands on the calculation. He said he would calculate it again, and would send Halley a copy. In November he did so, and in December sent the Royal Society a short book on the subject.

With that, Halley went back to Newton and said essentially, "Newton, you just sit down and write out what's in your head. Don't worry about the arrangements. I'll take care of everything." Within eighteen months, Newton had written the *Principia,* the Mathematical Principles of Natural Philosophy, held by many to be the greatest scientific work ever written.

I want to read you a passage from Newton's *Opticks.* He had written the *Opticks* and put it away in a drawer for some thirty years. He is said to have been waiting for Hooke, the secretary of the Royal Society, to die. Hooke died in 1703; and in 1704 out came the *Opticks.* In its second edition, in 1717, Newton had added, at the end, a series of "Queries." They were things that he was not prepared to say, since he couldn't prove them, but that he was ready to ask. Hence the "Queries" are put in the form, "Is it not true that . . . ?" Any scientist reading those "Queries" is aghast, for they come right into the physics of our time, and all in terms of Newton's profound intuitions, his intimacy with the universe, the things he felt pretty sure about, not through analysis, but by recognition, the way one knows a close friend.

I've marked a few places in the *Opticks* that I want to read you. Newton was a sober, withdrawn, almost—one would say—an austere person; but occasionally he was shaken by emotions that came out of realizing experiences and illuminations of the most fundamental kind. Then his language achieves a Biblical quality, as in: "In Summer, when the

Sun's light [is] strongest, I placed a prism at the Hole of the Window-shut ... so that its Axis might be parallel to the Axis of the World." (*Opticks*, bk. 1, pt. 1)

And this passage from Query 31: "God in the Beginning formed Matter in solid, massy, hard, impenetrable, movable Particles, of such Sizes and Figures, and with such other Properties, and in such proportion to Space, as most conduced to the End for which He formed them; and that these primitive Particles being Solids, are incomparably harder than any porous Bodies compounded of them; even so very hard, as never to wear or break in pieces; no ordinary power being able to divide what God Himself made one in the first Creation." That is, among other things, a fair description of what we now call our elementary particles.

And here an ecstatic outburst: "Whence is it that Nature doth nothing in Vain; and whence arises all that Order and Beauty which we see in the World?" (*Opticks*, bk. 3, pt. 1)

The word *beauty* has a quite special place in science and mathematics, calling attention to an order and harmony that one finds in nature and in some systematic exercises of human thought. Johannes Kepler antedated by three centuries Edna Millay in the line from her sonnet quoted above, with his aphorism, "Geometria est archetypus pulchritudinis mundi" (Geometry is the archetype of the world's beauty) (*Harmony of the World*, Augsburg, 1619). Consider the physicist Eugene Wigner's statement: "The observation that comes closest to an explanation for the mathematical concepts cropping up in physics which I know is Einstein's statement that the only physical theories which we are willing to accept are the beautiful ones. It stands to argue that the concepts of mathematics, which invite the exercise of so much wit, have the quality of beauty" (*Symmetries and Reflections*, Indiana Univ. Press, 1967, p. 229). And Richard Feynman's criterion for choosing among rival scientific theories, "Yes, we can recognize truth by its simplicity and by its beauty" (*Character of Physical Law*, MIT Press, 1967, p. 171). The Latin motto "Simplex sigillum veri" (The simple is the seal of the true) is inscribed in large letters in the physics auditorium of the University of Göttingen. And another Latin motto, "Pulchritudo splendor veritatis" (Beauty is the splendor of truth) (Werner Heisenberg, "The Meaning of Beauty in the Exact Sciences," in *Across the Frontiers*, Harper and

Row, 1974, p. 174). What one tries most to achieve in a scientific theory or mathematical argument is simplicity and beauty.

And now a great novelist drawing upon mathematical physics: Tolstoy divided his *War and Peace* into a number of parts, and in chapter 1 of each part discussed its contribution to his epic. Chapter 1 of part 1 brings us close again to Newton; for Newton in the *Principia* invented the calculus. (Simultaneously—or nearly so—it was invented also by Leibniz, causing a bitter controversy on who came first, a problem we can happily forego.)

Here Tolstoy appeals to the calculus. What has *War and Peace* to do with that? Well, throughout *War and Peace* Tolstoy is developing his theory of history: that history is not the outcome of decisions and commands of emperors and generals but is the outcome of the unplanned, unthinking movements of masses of people. What are called in retrospect the decisions of leaders, are in reality the gross and usually unpredictable results of those mass movements. The place of each individual in the mass is that of an infinitesimal in the differential calculus; and what emerges from the mass is the integral of those infinitesimal individual contributions.

So Tolstoy: "A new branch of mathematics dealing with infinitely small quantities gives now in problems of dynamics solutions of problems that seemed insoluble."

"This new branch of mathematics, unknown to the ancients, by assuming infinitely small quantities, that is, such as secure the chief condition of motion (absolute continuity), corrects the inevitable error which the human intellect cannot but make when it considers disconnected units of motion instead of continuous motion."

"In the investigation of the laws of historical motion precisely the same mistake arises."

"The progress of humanity, arising from an innumerable multitude of individual wills, is continuous in its motion."

"The discovery of the laws of this motion is the aim of history."

"Only by assuming an infinitely small unit for observation—a differential of history—that is, the homogeneous tendencies of men, and arriving at the integral calculus (that is, taking the sum of those infinitesimal quantities), can we hope to arrive at the laws of history."

Every art form has its own language, is indeed that language. Therein lies for me a frustration in my academic environment; for too frequently the university, rather than letting the arts speak for themselves, turns them all into *words:* interpretation, history, criticism, verbal exposition. One sometimes asks the artists themselves to say in prose what they *mean* by their productions. But if they could say it in prose, why paint, or sculpt, or say it as a poem?

I want to tell you of an episode in the language of painting. Perhaps I should warn you that doing so will be in a sense an aggression, for I rather think that, as has happened to me, you'll never be able to forget it; you'll never be quite the same again.

I had a friend, Vladimir Gurewich, a heart specialist. One day, as we were walking together, he said to me, "You know, I have a hobby—the iconography of Christ. All the major details in the representation of Christ are set by tradition, and the artist has to work within that tradition. So in paintings of the crucifixion, the wound in the body of Christ was always on the right side, up until about 1630. Then, all at once, it moved to the left side. I don't know who moved it first, but both Rembrandt and Rubens painted it on the left side at just about that time." And then—a heart specialist!—he added, "You know, that's just about the time that William Harvey wrote *The Circulation of the Blood* (1628). I wonder whether that shifted the interest from the right side to the left, where the heart is." (cf. Vladimir Gurewich, "Observations of the Iconography of the Wound in Christ's Side," *Journal of the Warburg and Courtauld Institute* 20 (1957): 358–62.)

Ever since that conversation I cannot see a Crucifixion or a pietà without quickly looking to see whether the wound is on the right side or the left. I'm afraid that from now on that will be your fate too. In my own experience, up to early in the seventeenth century it's always on the right side. After that it's almost always on the left, with only an occasional exception. It's interesting that in the old colonial churches in Mexico or the American southwest, I have found it continuing on the right side much later, probably because the artists went on taking their iconographic cues from earlier paintings and sculptures brought over from Spain.

Nature abounds in mysteries. Some are just puzzles that one hopes to work out. Some others are quite awesome, stirring the imagination and the emotions. One of the privileges of being a scientist is to know where they are, and to let oneself dream about them.

I had the joy of knowing two of that monumental generation of physicists who filled the first half of this century. They worked not only with but upon one another; so that each of them became something more than any of them could have been by himself. The two I knew were Albert Einstein and Niels Bohr. They were at once the greatest and most childlike persons I have ever encountered. There were no fences around them. Their curiosity was boundless. They were eagerly interested in everything interesting. They used to make me think of a man walking with a puppy. The man walks a straight line, but the puppy is into everything, every corner. That's how it was with Einstein and Bohr.

Once to my great surprise Bohr began to talk about the migrations of the eels, the so-called freshwater eels, *Anguilla*. All the eels along the shores of the North Atlantic, both European and American, leave fresh water at sexual maturity and migrate to the Sargasso Sea. There, at great depths, they shed their eggs and sperm and die. The young larval eels have to find their way back alone. The European and American eels are different species, and there is as yet no record of a larval eel going to the wrong continent. It takes the American larvae about fifteen months to come to our shores and ascend our rivers. It takes the European larvae about three years to get back home. How do they find their way back? No one has any idea. Bohr said of this something utterly wonderful. He said: "It is just because they do not know where they are going that they always do it perfectly."

To me that is the most profound commentary on that fateful episode in the Garden of Eden. If that had been a Greek story, the tree that provided the forbidden fruit would have been the Tree of Knowledge. But it was a Jewish story; hence, in accord with the Jewish obsession with sin, that tree became the Tree of the Knowledge of Good and Evil. I think that what Bohr was saying is that animals are guarded by their instincts, by ways built into their structures and behavior by their evolution. Human beings, having eaten of the forbidden fruit, have lost the safeguards of instinctual life and are free to choose, for good or ill. That has special meaning for us now that we are facing an apocalypse. We have made wrong choices; and after three billion years of life on the Earth, some three million years of something like human life, and some ten thousand years of civilization, a mere two hundred years of our high-technology industrial society have brought the human species to the brink of extinction, the first self-extinction in the history of life on this planet. That could be the result of a nuclear war for which all the armaments are already stockpiled.

It is no accident that our Bible begins with a cosmology. So do all other bibles; and all religions, however "primitive," have a cosmology at their base, that colors the entire culture.

It is interesting in that regard that both the Greco-Roman and the ever-so-much-more-ancient Hindu mythologies divide human history into four stages, deteriorating continuously from an initially perfect state. The Greco-Roman tradition takes us, as you know, from a Golden Age, to a Silver, a Bronze, and at last an Iron Age—*our* Age. Similarly the Hindus divide our history into four stages called *Yugas,* starting with the perfect Yuga called Krita, which is four-square; then Treta (all our Indo-European languages come out of Sanskrit. Treta is three: only three quarters of perfection left); then Dvapara (*two,* as in double: two quarters left, so half-gone); and finally the Kali Yuga, *our* Yuga, named for Kali, the goddess of destruction and dissolution. (One may take some comfort in realizing that in both traditions the first three stages are mythological; only the last stage is historical.)

In the Hindu tradition the final dissolution is only to prepare for the next cycle, the rebirth: Brahma sleeps, but he will reawaken and dream a new universe. But our Judeo-Christian is a one-shot religion: one universe, one life (in the flesh). Our self-destruction would be irrevocable.

What we have in both these traditions, and in our own that begins in the Garden of Eden, is in a sense a mythological perception of the operation of our Second Law of Thermodynamics, the concept that what began as a wound-up universe is continuously running down; that throughout the universe free energy—energy capable of doing work—is being degraded, ultimately to heat, entropy, completely disorganized energy, from which, if at one level of temperature, no further work can be extracted. (Hence Hell must be at one temperature; for if there were a difference of temperatures in Hell, one could use it to work a refrigerator.) This is the concept that inspired Lord Kelvin's portentous phrase "the heat death of the universe." And what—some would ask Who—wound the universe up? An uncomfortable question for physicists, a consolation to fundamentalist Judeo-Christians. Is it indeed a cyclic universe? And if so, what would bring it back each swing to the same initial state? For unless it came all the way back each time, the cycles must gradually run down, bringing us back again to that uncomfortable question.

I have spoken of Newton's two years of rustication, during which he seems to have figured out the universe. Ancient Hindus seem to have done the same. They attached a chronology to the Yugas that invokes lengths of time that present science has caught up with only in the last forty or fifty years. According to one computation the Kali Yuga—*ours*—began on Friday, February 18, 3102 B.C., not very far from where we might now date the beginnings of urbanization. All four Yugas add up to make a Great Yuga (Mahayuga) of 4,320,000 years—not far from the beginnings of man-like creatures. One thousand Mahayugas make a Kaupa, one day of Brahma; that is 4.32 billion years, close to the age of our Earth, now set at about 4.8 billion years.

Compare these numbers with the 5,741 years of the Hebrew calendar, that learned men in our culture only two centuries ago were still trying to defend. How did the ancient Hindus perceive a chronology that our Western science has only lately discovered? An interesting question. Rustication may have helped there too; and an associated respect for and veneration of nature that would have thought puerile the idea that it had been created technologically in six days.

I should like now to speak of how our own present cosmology affects our views of nature and life and the human condition. Let me first say that I taught at Harvard—God help me—for forty-three years, stopping just four years ago. For the last sixteen of those years I gave the beginning course in our Biology Department. I think I am the first person in the history of Harvard to *volunteer* to give the Freshman course. It was just what I wanted to do. I have my specialty, the chemistry and physiology of vision. This permitted me a second scientific life, with the great questions that a bright child might ask, and that are never finished answering. I thought of my own lectures in that course as "From Hydrogen to Hamlet." So let me go as quickly as I can, beginning with hydrogen, and hoping to still leave a little time for Hamlet.

We know now that we live in a historical universe, one in which not only living organisms but stars and galaxies are born, come to maturity, grow old, and die. It is, I think, a universe permeated with life, in which life arises, given enough time, wherever the conditions exist that make it possible. How many such places are there? Well, I like Arthur Eddington's old formula: 10^{11} stars (10^{11} is one hundred billion)—10^{11} stars make a galaxy; 10^{11} galaxies make a universe. That formula holds rather well. Our own galaxy, the Milky Way, contains about one hundred billion stars. You must try to take that in. We now have something over four billion persons on the Earth and some of us are beginning to feel crowded. But our own home galaxy, the Milky Way, has one hundred billion stars like our Sun. It's a vast thing, so vast that light, traveling at 186,000 miles per second, takes about one hundred thousand years just to cross the Milky Way.

I have heard the possibility denied that there are creatures like us in outer space on the grounds, "Then why aren't they here? Why haven't they visited us?" I think the simplest answer is, why come here?—why, with one hundred billion stars to choose among, come here? It's like denying that someone named Swenson lives in Stockholm because there are ships and planes; why isn't he here? The answer is that he didn't choose to come here! (The galactic question has also a further answer: he couldn't come, however advanced his technology, even if he chose. The distances are too great, even if one could travel at the speed of light; and it's hard to do that without *being* light. So no interstellar visiting.)

The lowest estimate I have ever seen for the fraction of stars in our galaxy that should have a planet that can bear life is one percent. That means one billion such places just in the Milky Way; and with about one billion such galaxies already within view of our telescopes, the lowest estimate we are offered for the number of inhabited planets in the already observed universe is of the order of one billion billion, 10^{18}.

May I add that in our own solar system the only life is that on the Earth. That is indeed the rule: the overwhelming likelihood is for any solar system in the universe to contain only one planet that possesses the environment—the size, temperature, distance from its sun—that permits life to arise. We are asked to believe that there may be life elsewhere in the solar system only to help reconcile us to the huge sums of tax money that go into space exploration. But that money is devoted mainly, not to finding life elsewhere, but to destroying life here. The major interest in space programs, from their inception and increasingly now, is military: the remote control and guidance systems, the photographic and communications technology, the orbiting satellites and space shuttle, all represent primarily military ventures.

One can most readily conceive of beginning our universe with hydrogen, the smallest of the elements. Each hydrogen atom is composed of one proton as nucleus and one satellite electron. Surely large parts of this universe, if not the whole of it, started as a mass of hydrogen filling a large section of space. Then, over the ages, just by chance—chance of course governs all that happens in the universe—an eddy, a somewhat denser aggregate of hydrogen occurs, which if big enough begins to draw in the hydrogen about it through the ordinary forces of gravitation. So it grows, and the more of it there is, the better it is at pulling in the hydrogen about it. So we have a growing, collapsing mass of hydrogen; and as it collapses—as anything collapses—it heats up. When the temperature in the deep interior reaches five million degrees, something new begins to happen. The nuclei of the hydrogen atoms, the protons, begin to fuse to helium nuclei: four protons, each of mass 1, fusing to form a helium nucleus of mass about 4. But in this transaction a tiny bit of mass is lost; four protons have a slightly larger mass than a helium nucleus. That tiny bit of lost mass is turned into radiation (including sunlight!) according to Einstein's beautifully simple formula, $E = mc^2$, in which E is the energy of the radiation, m the bit of lost mass, and c is a tremendous number, the speed of light, 3×10^{10} cm/sec. Squaring that big number yields a truly prodigious number, big enough to convert even the tiniest mass into a huge amount of radiation. That radiation, poured out in the interior of what had been a collapsing mass of hydrogen, backs up the further collapse. A star has been born, to take its place, as we say, on the Main Sequence.

A Main Sequence star lives by this process of fusing hydrogen to helium. So a time must come to every such star when it begins to run short of hydrogen. Hence it produces less radiation and so begins to collapse again. With that it heats up some more. When the temperature in the interior reaches about one hundred million degrees, something new again begins to happen. This time it's the helium nuclei that begin to fuse, each of mass 4. It's all simple arithmetic. Two heliums fuse: 4 + 4 make 8—that's beryllium 8, a nucleus so unstable that it disintegrates almost instantly. Yet in these enormous masses of material there are always a few beryllium nuclei, and here and there one of them captures another helium: 8 + 4 make 12, and 12 is the mass of a carbon atom. That is the way in which carbon enters our universe. Then carbon can capture another helium: 12 + 4 = 16; and that's oxygen. Carbon can also pick up hydrogen nuclei; so carbon 12 plus two hydrogens make 14, and that's nitrogen. That is how oxygen and nitrogen are formed in our universe. These new processes result in a new outpouring of radiation that not only stops the star from collapsing further but puffs it up to enormous size. It becomes a Red Giant— a dying star.

Such Red Giants are in a delicate condition. They keep spewing their substance out into space to become part of the masses of gases and dust that fill all interstellar space. Then here and there, over the ages, an eddy forms in the gases and dust, a somewhat higher concentration, that if big enough begins to draw in the gases and dust around it through the ordinary forces of gravitation; and so a new star is born. But such later-generation stars, unlike the first generation that was composed wholly of hydrogen and helium—those later-generation stars contain also carbon and nitrogen and oxygen. And we know that our Sun is such a later-generation star *because we're here*—because we, along with all the other living creatures we know—and I think I could prove to you, given another talk, that that is how it has to be wherever life arises in the universe—we, and I think all other life, are composed almost wholly of just those four elements I have discussed. Ninety-nine percent of our living substance is made of hydrogen, oxygen, nitrogen, and carbon. It is a moving realization that stars in dying create elements that permit organisms to live.

We live in a remarkably integrated universe. Those four elements that form life on the planets also generate sunlight in the stars by fusing hydrogen to helium in an alternative way, not by direct fusion but by a catalytic carbon cycle: carbon 12 + 2 hydrogens = nitrogen 14, which by adding two more hydrogens = carbon 12 + helium 4. And then—ultimate benison—the life comes to run on the sunlight. Life could never have been able to persist on the Earth, nor could it on any other planet, without inventing the process of photosynthesis, whereby, using the energy of sunlight, plants make all the organic molecules (those composed of hydrogen, oxygen, nitrogen, and carbon) that living things require. For several billion years all life on the Earth has run on photosynthesis, on sunlight.

A planet that bears life, and its sun, form in a sense one organism, sharing one metabolism based upon the same four elements. It has to be that way, for of the ninety-two natural elements those four have unique properties not shared with any other elements. Living things depend upon those properties in the molecules ("organic") that those elements compose; and stars depend upon the special properties of their nuclei.

Life seems to represent the most complex state of organization that matter achieves in our universe. It possesses another extraordinary property: individuality. The very definition of a *substance* in chemistry is that all its molecules are identical; but I doubt that there are in the entire universe two identical organisms. Even the simplest of them, witness those now famous *E. coli* that populate our large intestine, though they look identical under an ordinary light microscope, need only an electron microscope to show that they are all different. It is not only that every living organism differs from every other; it differs also from itself from moment to moment. It is a wholly dynamic entity in both form and substance, the locus of a continuous flow of matter and energy. That is its life. When that stops the organism is at least dormant and more likely dead.

We human beings add a new dimension to life on the Earth. We are those creatures that know and create. Much of the history of the universe is bound up in our substance. The carbon, nitrogen, and oxygen of which we are principally composed were cooked in the deep interiors of earlier generations of dying stars. The waters of ancient seas flow in our veins—more dilute than sea water is now because ever since the time hundreds of millions of years ago when the blood circulation first closed off portions of sea water, the rivers have been carrying further salts into the seas.

Human beings and their like are a great event whenever and wherever they appear in the universe. I say "and their like" because I see no escape from the thought that in many other places in this highly populated universe there must exist other such contemplative, science-, art-, and technology-making animals. Yet not men; not of our species, genus, perhaps not even of our class or phylum. To achieve homo sapiens anywhere else in the universe would mean repeating the entire extent of evolution there exactly as it has run off here; and that seems to me as improbable as I can imagine. So I think there are many other such thinking, making, knowing creatures in many other places, some probably far ahead of us in all these ways—but not *men*. I think we are the only human beings in the universe.

In the knowing of all such creatures, as in our knowing, the universe begins to know itself. I have heard it said that a hen is only an egg's way of making another egg. In much the same sense a human being is the atom's way of knowing about atoms; the star's way of knowing about stars: a great and wonderful thing.

I used to tell those Freshman students of mine that I hoped they would come out of my course proud and angry—proud of what it could and should mean to be human; and angry that the conditions of their lives kept them so far short of realizing those proud potentialities. For these last two hundred years since the Industrial Revolution have been disastrous to the human enterprise. We have substituted production for creation. We are not only threatening now to exterminate the human species—that unique creature—but we have largely forgotten what we are—how to dream, how to play, how to love. For those aspects of life have no industrial uses; they are only in the way.

Let me conclude by trying to tell you some of my own thoughts about the human condition and some of its potentialities. In the Boston Museum of Fine Arts there is a magnificent painting by Gauguin out of his South Seas period. In the upper left corner he has lettered the questions: "D'oú venons nous? Que sommes nous? Oú allons nous?" Those are the perennial questions that we will never finish answering. What I want to say now touches upon them. It is strange that though I am a biologist, it is easier to say what I am going to to physicists, particularly those working at the frontiers of physics.

I think that we're in a period in which not only our concept of what it is to be human, but our concept of what it is to be a scientist is being degraded. I take enormous comfort in that monumental generation of physicists, the last of whom died recently. They were acutely conscious of what science is about, holding views of it that go back not only to Newton but to long before what we now call science existed. For I believe, and I think they did too, that science is ultimately a religious vocation. I mean the word religious in the widest sense, lacking a better word. Science tries to approach the ultimate questions about reality—what it is, what place matter, the universe, life, human life have in that reality. One cannot deal with the whole of reality within science, only with a select part of it; and as all major scientists have always known and often said, the smaller part. I think that the greatest privilege in being a scientist is that it leads one to the boundaries of what science can explore, so that one knows where the great mysteries begin, where to begin to look beyond those boundaries.

I have spent my scientific life mainly working on mechanisms of vision, what light does in eyes, eyes of every kind. When I began, it was a lonely field; but now science is so well supplied with federal funds that we are told that there are more scientists at work now than have existed in the whole of earlier human history. That once lonely field of mine is now crowded. The last time I went to the annual meeting held in Sarasota devoted to just that little corner of the field of vision, twenty-four hundred workers turned up, all eager to give papers.

What with all this activity, we have learned a lot, and expect to learn much more. But for me, in the background from the beginning was a disturbing realization. Now it is in the foreground. It is that one can put together everything we have learned and all that anyone hopes to learn, and none of it comes close to or even points in the direction of *what it means to see.* Let me say that more plainly. When I work on the visual mechanisms of frogs and of human beings, I come out with very much the same answers. The molecules involved, their reactions, the nerve pathways are all much the same. But I know that I see. Does a frog see? It reacts to light. So do garage doors and all kinds of photoelectric devices. But does it know, is it aware that it is reacting? There is nothing, zero, that I can do as a scientist to answer that question.

That is the problem of consciousness; and what I have just said is that it lies outside science. I can do nothing as a scientist to identify its presence *or its absence.* All my assumptions of the presence or absence of consciousness in structures other than ourselves are just that—unsupported assumptions. I tend to believe that mammals are conscious; I don't know what to think about frogs, still less fish, much less the worms and scallops whose eyes I have worked on. I can do nothing to verify my beliefs and doubts. When a computer beats a human player at chess, is it elated? Nothing I can do about that either. (It may be objected that the computer was programmed by a person; but wasn't also the chess player?)

How comforting it would be at this pass to be able to dismiss consciousness as an illusion, an epiphenomenon; as the physicist P. W. Bridgman once said to me, as "just a way of talking." He said that because he had stated the criterion of reality to be the operations available to define it. There are no operations available for defining consciousness.

But consciousness is not just an epiphenomenon. It is basic, our only perception of reality. No consciousness, no science. Every proper physicist knows that and deals with it constantly. Consciousness still embarrasses biologists, for they think that since it is a characteristic of at least some living organisms, they ought to know how to handle it, even know to tell physicists how to handle it. What irony! For physicists live day in and day out with the awareness of the basic role of consciousness in modern physics. One of those past, monumental physicists, Wolfgang Pauli (the exclusion principle) said: "Psyche and Physics are the two complementary aspects of the same reality." He was talking *complementarity,* a concept proposed by Niels Bohr to deal, at least verbally, with the realization that we regularly, in and out of science, encounter phenomena that possess mutually incompatible sets of properties that one nevertheless has to accept and live with.

The most familiar example in physics, and the one to which Bohr first applied the principle of complementarity, is the realization that light—as indeed all the other elementary particles—presents us with properties both of waves and particles, always one or the other but never both, since those properties are mutually incompatible. And now, enter consciousness: the experimenter chooses beforehand which set of properties he will encounter, wave or particle. If he sets up a wave experiment, he gets a wave answer; from a particle experiment he gets a particle answer. Hence what Pauli said is that physical phenomena and our perception of them in consciousness are complementary aspects of the same reality, one as acceptable as the other.

When I say that consciousness lies beyond the operations of science, is that just a temporary state, an inadequacy of present technique that some day will be repaired? No, I think it is forever, in the nature of things. In that regard it is like Heisenberg's uncertainty principle, which states the limits within which one cannot specify simultaneously the velocity and the position of a particle. It is commonly conceded now that that is not a confession of technical inadequacy, but a statement of the nature of physical reality: the particle *does not possess* simultaneously an accurate position and velocity. I think that consciousness will always remain impervious to science and to its classic parameters of space and time.

Science is often spoken of as the endless frontier. It is bounded only by an ever-receding horizon. However high science ascends, the horizon retreats further. When I speak of the boundaries of science, I mean that horizon receding without limit. But a still larger reality stretches like the sky above that sea of science and is itself endless.

In the course of my scientific life I have encountered two problems which, though rooted in science, though they would occur in this form only to a scientist, project beyond science, and are I think ultimately insoluble as science. One I have already discussed, the problem of consciousness. The other is equally evasive. It is the problem of cosmology, how the universe came to be as it is. For this is a very special universe, and a biologist above all should know that.

For we find ourselves in a universe that breeds life; and that requires a quite particular order of universe, one with a special constellation of properties. Some of those properties seem basic, others trivial, almost accidental. Yet if any one of them were otherwise, we would have a universe that should be workable and stable, but lifeless. From our somewhat prejudiced point of view, what we have is the best way to construct a universe. What I want to know is: how did the universe find that out?

Some of those special properties are astonishingly familiar. The most important molecule for life—indeed irreplaceable—is water. Water is also the strangest molecule in the whole of chemistry; and its strangest property is that *ice floats*. If ice did not float, I doubt that life would exist in the universe.

All of you know that on cooling, things contract. That's how we make thermometers: we put a thread of mercury or alcohol into a capillary tube on a scale. On cooling, either fluid contracts, and we read the temperature. Virtually everything contracts on cooling. So does water, down to four degrees centigrade. Then, between four and zero degrees centigrade, where it freezes, it expands so greatly that the ice, when it forms, is lighter than water and so floats. If it were not for that extraordinary expansion below four degrees centigrade, water would grow heavier and heavier as it cools. The colder water would always be sinking to the bottom. Freezing would begin, not as now at the surface, but at the bottom of the water; and as it went on, the water would freeze all the way through. That would be the end of anything living in it; for a big enough mass of ice takes endlessly to thaw. If there were just one ice age in a million years on any inhabited planet, that would be the end of its life; and if life on that planet were in the slow process of forming, it would get no further.

There are other such properties, some of them equally aberrant. How is it that the proton and electron, otherwise so altogether different, have a numerically identical electric charge? The elements (hydrogen, oxygen, nitrogen, and carbon) that primarily compose life—as also the stars!—possess unique properties not shared with any other elements. And on and on.

We find ourselves in a life-breeding universe. Out of many options, this one has come about. If it weren't that way, there would be no one to find out. And that, perhaps, is why it *is* that way.

A short time ago it struck me (strange phrase!), at first with some shock to my scientific sensibilities, that my two major problems, both, as I believe, forever insoluble as science, might at least be brought into relation with each other. This is with the thought that consciousness, instead of being, as I and all other biologists have supposed, a late product in the evolution of life, on the contrary was there always and is indeed the source of the material universe. The reason we find ourselves in a universe that breeds life is that consciousness, mind, designed it that way, so that eventually, through living creatures such as human beings, the material universe might come to know and understand itself.

The shock is there again as I say those words. Have I said them too plainly? Yet I think they have their uses, even to scientists who might repudiate them. They invite examining what science is really about, and what are its limits—an examination that has been going on intensively throughout this century. And they call into question an important and commonly shared preconception.

I have explained that science is unable to deal with consciousness, even to identify its presence or absence. Yet strangely enough almost all biologists and even almost all of those enlightened physicists who have had most to deal with consciousness have taken it for granted that consciousness has a location, that it is in the brain. Yet consciousness is not a phenomenon to be placed in space or time. There is no basis whatever for locating it.

I used to talk about this with Wilder Penfield, the great Canadian neurosurgeon. He had been seeking, as he seemed to have unique opportunities to do, the location of the organ of consciousness within the human brain. I asked him, "Why do you think it's in the brain?" He chuckled and said, "Well, I'll keep on trying." The next time I met him he said, "Well,

I'll tell you one thing. It's not in the cerebral cortex!" A few years later there was some excitement among neurophysiologists involving an area of the brain within the so-called reticular formation that acts as an arousal center, a center for awareness. All such instances face a dilemma: is one dealing with a source, or just part of the instrumentation?—as if one removed one of the tubes or transistors from a TV set and, finding that it didn't communicate any longer, concluded that part to be the source of the program.

Erwin Schrödinger, who invented the wave mechanics, announced in the last chapter of his book *What is Life?* that he had for many years taken a deep interest in Eastern mysticism. Then he raised such questions as, Are we not perhaps mistaken in assuming that there are as many minds as there are bodies? Clearly there are many bodies, yet perhaps many fewer minds; perhaps, indeed, only *one* mind.

Yes, perhaps ultimately only one mind. Perhaps we are a little more than we suppose like those TV sets. Do they know that they are communicating? I think not; but there is nothing I can do to be sure.

Surely it's time I stopped. So thank you.

MAXINE KUMIN: Well, we are a great many bodies here. Shall we see if we are one mind? Is there someone who would like to—yes. Here's a hand. Wendell?

WENDELL BERRY: I have a couple of questions to help myself to understand. If there is nothing but consciousness, which you suggested at one point, then there is a serious question of whether or not there is anything but consciousness, is that right?

WALD: Well, I was suggesting that it was not the material world that bred consciousness but consciousness that bred the material world.

BERRY: Then my question is, If consciousness is at the source, or is everything, how can it be insufficient or in error? And another question is, if chance governs everything, which I think you said—

WALD: Yes.

BERRY: Then what is the role of responsibility?

WALD: Your first question, if consciousness is everything, how can it make mistakes? If I understand the point of your question, it involves the problem of what we speak of frequently as the problem of good and evil, right? Now, all the Eastern religions realize that those also are two complementary aspects of reality, the good and the evil. There is no Eastern god who has not the aspects of both creation and destruction built into him. And I think that the problem is a Judeo-Christian one in being told that we're dealing with a good and loving God, the universal creator, though here and there mention is made of an evil spirit called Satan. Now, I think several things, and please forgive me if I seem sacrilegious. I think first of all that if you read the introductory portions of the Book of Job, they describe a very cozy relationship between God and Satan, and—Alan Watts notes—I think in his book *Beyond Theology*—that we have been told who sits on the right hand of God, but who sits on his left hand? Pretty surely, that must be Satan. And you know—I'm Jewish, and please forgive me for taking liberties—I've always wondered about the composition of the Christian Trinity—the Father, the Son, and the Spirit, the Holy Ghost. Surely the Father must possess the Spirit. Why divide it off? What can that mean? I've never understood that. And it would make much more sense to me, I must say, to have Alan Watts's Trinity, Father, Son, and Satan. Then one doesn't have the problem of evil any more, which is just, if you wish, the absence of good or the counter of good and an intrinsic part of reality.

Now, you had a second question. It was about chance. You see, everything that happens does so because there's a chance of its happening. And chance is in essence a very simple thing. All probability runs from zero: 0.00000, which is the impossible—the technically impossible—to 1.—exactly 1, which is the certain. And everything that happens in the world fits on this tiny scale (tiny if drawn arithmetically) between 0 and 1. I don't quite understand what trouble that gives you.

JERRY POURNELLE: How can you have a responsibility if it's just plain chance; if it's just the blind workings of chance, how can you hold anyone morally responsible for anything? Many times, during your speech, you obviously held large portions of people, the people in this government, for instance, as morally responsible for actions which you also attribute to chance.

WALD: No. You see, a human being is something that starts genetically and then begins to accumulate a history. And the genetics and the physiology and the history is all that person. There is no reason in the world why one should refuse to accord responsibility to that person as one finds him or her. I believe that free will exists, but in a deterministic world. I think, myself, that free will is not a failure of determinism but, on the contrary, a failure of predictability. My free will consists in the fact that you don't entirely know what I'm going to do next; but when I've done it, I think I can be held responsible with perfect justice. The determinism is so obscure, the predictability so impossible, that it seems to me the responsibility is something that is part of that individual.

JAMES BEALL: Let me raise a question. You said that there is nothing that we can do to identify the presence or absence of consciousness. Now, if science is the investigation of the material world and literature is the investigation of an interior landscape, and we're here to investigate the connections between the two, based on that statement, should we all go home now?

WALD: Not at all. But, as I say, having spent my life with vision, this is a hardly avoidable problem for me—and, you see, all that I can do is go from the physics and chemistry of the world outside my skin to the physics and chemistry of the world *inside* my skin. Your question implies that I have ruled out consciousness from reality. But just the opposite: it is the primary reality. Everything else, including all science, is derivative. All the science and all the literature come together in *my* (and *your*) consciousness. So no need to go home; that's how it is there too.

BERRY: There's nothing implicit in the nature of reality as you understand it that says we shouldn't destroy it.

WALD: On the contrary. You see, some of my physicist friends are starry-eyed over the prospect of coming into radio communication with what they describe as superior technological societies in outer space. I myself think that's another nightmare. We don't need to go into that, but nightmare or not, they've been listening now for a generation without hearing anything meaningful. And so, the idea has come up and is beginning to spread: perhaps there *are* no superior technological societies in outer space. Perhaps they exterminate themselves when they reach about our stage, as we are now threatening to do. Now, let me say that I reject this sort of thinking root and branch. I refuse to believe that there is any kind of natural law operating that necessarily puts so disastrous an end to a, let me call it, humanoid society. I think this has resulted from the peculiar structure of our particular society; and I would do everything I could to change it. And I still have hope for human survival, though any sensible person would realize that it becomes less likely every day.

KUMIN: Could I just interject to speak up for the poets? I'm sure you will remember John Ciardi's book of poems, it must be twenty years ago, called *As If*, and the prevailing thesis of that was that we must live our lives as if there's a chance, as if there is some certitude, as if there is a possibility of pursuing the morality of survival, of love, and so on, to ensure that life goes on.

GENE RODDENBERRY: Just to extend the question about the nature of chance in the universe. Was the bomb that was dropped on Nagasaki a chance event?

WALD: Everything that happens is a chance event. That is, one could have had some busy people calculating the probabilities that involved, among other things, that Mr. Truman would decide, yeah, we'll drop that bomb. There was a lot of controversy going on, it was nothing that one could give a flat answer to, one would have had to compute the probabilities. Having done that, one would still have had to await the outcome, the event itself.

POURNELLE: You are telling me you know how to compute the probability of a single unique event?

WALD: Not at all. As I said earlier, I think that our entire conviction of exercising what we call free will involves no failure of determinism but only a failure of predictability—except in a statistical sense. But that lack of predictability of the unique event of course involves all physics. Physical law is statistical. That's what Heisenberg's uncertainty principle is about. Electrons, atoms, and people—one can assign probabilities for their behavior but never can say what the individual will do, or at what moment.

MYRA SKLAREW: I'd like to take a bit of a turn and ask Dr. MacLean, in his work on the archaeology of the brain, whether he thinks of consciousness as early or late, and whether he would locate it any place?

PAUL DONALD MacLEAN: Well, the only answer I can give to that is that if you start whittling away at the cerebral hemispheres, both animals and humans become not very interesting once you get beyond the mid-brain, so I sort of feel that there's some sort of consciousness in the cerebral hemispheres.

WALD: Oh, they're very useful.

MacLEAN: About your hard particles of Newton, how do you believe anything that this soft avocado-brain tells us? That's my problem. We're living in such a closed-in, private world, how can we ever have any faith that these myriad sticky cells, which function God knows how, how can we believe any of that stuff? What's light, I mean? You've been spending all your life with light, but that may be an artifact of the neocortex or something like that.

WALD: On believing that, you check it out all the time and, you know, still make mistakes. It happens all the time.

BEALL: If I could interject a point, Descartes worried about this, and didn't get anywhere, either.

RODDENBERRY: It seemed to me that he suggested an answer to some of these questions in the "one mind" concept, and I took it to mean that perhaps, as these organisms evolve to a certain point, they get in contact and begin to make use of this one mind. And it struck me that how perfectly or imperfectly they are in contact and make use may answer many of these questions of right and wrong and chance and so on. Does that seem to follow?

WALD: Yes. T. S. Eliot, in *Murder in the Cathedral,* speaks of—the quotation's gone out of my head—"to do the right thing for the wrong reason." The right thing for the wrong reason. That's human talk. Animals don't—you see, we are the unique animals on this planet that talk all the time while we act. We're constantly explaining as we act. You put any number of organisms into some dark box, then you turn on the light at the end. Some organisms stream toward the light; some organisms stream away from the light. But they're not talking, OK? Hence, we say, ah yes, those that go toward are positively phototropic and those that come away are negatively phototropic. And then you have organisms that sort of go back and forth, and you can write a lot of Ph.D. theses about these things. Now, the curious thing is, you imagine, just imagine that this room were completely darkened, and we were left in it as a completely dark room with the realization that we're not in control at all. There's some people, forces outside there that are running things, OK? And all at once, a light opens right there in that corner; what do we do? Well, if we're not too afraid of those outside forces, we're probably going to go to that light as fast as we can in the hope that's the way of getting out, or at least looking out. Then someone says, "Aha, positively phototropic." That's a lot of crap, isn't it? It has nothing to do with phototropism, it's you, figuring things. But you're announcing that immediately. A guy says "positively phototropic." You tell him, "Hell, no, I was hoping that would be an open door." Or if they feared sufficiently they might cower in a corner, but talking all the time, explaining all the time. So it is a very curious situation. We're the only animals that explain our actions as we act, and if a psychiatrist is present, or a psychoanalyst, he'll probably be saying, "Don't believe what that guy's saying, that's just stuff."

VICTOR KUMIN: Professor Wald, I'm interested in your example of the eels. I don't know whether you used the word *instinct* there or not, but a general summation of your description of the American eels coming to the American coast and the European eels always going back to the European coast, I got out of that the word *instinct;* that for some reason this is an instinct of the eels to return, without any guidance system that we know of that forces them in those directions, and yet you implied that man has no instinct, if I understood you correctly. And if I misunderstood that, do you think that there is an instinct in man for self-destruction, just as there is an instinct in the eels to proceed east or west, depending on their origins? This always-downhill process that you talked about?

WALD: No, I think the instinct in man in general is for survival, and we take self-destructiveness as psychopathic; something terribly wrong, if not psychopathic. No, I think we are filled with animal instincts which, however, we frequently override, treat with violence, and so on. Let me give you a simple example. Just about any mammal you choose would live in the following way if it had free access to food and water. It sleeps for awhile, it wakes up and begins to run, and then it comes back and eats, drinks, and then it goes to sleep, and then it runs, and then it eats, and then it sleeps, and it goes through the whole day in such a cycle. It takes mammals about four hours, this cycle. Now, a professor at Johns Hopkins years ago, Kurt Rister, studied this in rats and then he thought, "Well, how is it in humans?" And so (those were the days when medical students were the cheapest experimental animals you could find) he got a group of medical students to let him experiment on them. The medical students had the extraordinary privilege of being given a bed in the laboratory. Before going to bed, they swallowed a balloon at the end of a tube, and the tube let out and registered on a drum all the motions of their stomachs. And the bed itself was very carefully balanced so any motion of the bed would be registered on the drum. Well, all through the night, in sleeping medical students, in a four-hour cycle, the stomach, having been very quiet, would begin to rise up into these slow, deep, so-called "hunger contractions," and as they reached a peak, the medical students would begin to toss around in the bed, which was registering; then the contractions would quiet down, the medical student would quiet down; four hours later he was back at that again. But, you see, when he's awake, he's violating all of this. We commit violence to this all the time, and one of the most awful things that happens to me now and then is to be asked to speak after a big dinner to a group of people who have just had a big dinner. Now, the right thing to do after a big dinner is to go to sleep. And there I am, struggling to try to keep the audience awake, you see. Well, that's all wrong. What do we do with a baby? As quickly as possible, we sort of force that baby into the pattern of an eight-hour day. But the baby starts at a four-hour cycle, and anyone who has lived with a baby knows that a baby waking up starts writhing and shouting and turning red and all kinds of things, and then you begin a feeding, and, gee, in my experience, you have to keep patting the kid's behind in order to just keep it awake long enough to finish the feeding, because then it's asleep again. But we promptly go to work on that baby and, as quickly as possible, put it on an eight-hour day. So what I am saying is yes, those animal instincts are there, but we take over.

BERRY: It seems to me that a lot of these questions we're dealing with here can be helped out by the fact that we can make mistakes in questions about the primacy of consciousness, in questions about the role of instinct, the question about responsibility. Such questions all have to do with the fact that you can make mistakes, and you seem to be implying that animals don't make mistakes, but they do.

WALD: Sure they do, sure they do; but, you see, the mistakes have been through a long process of weeding out. You know, extinction in the wild is still a rather deep and difficult biological problem. One is told answers for it that most of us think by now are just jokes, in a way, you know. Why is the Irish elk extinct? Because its antlers grew so wide that it couldn't run through the forests anymore. Now, everything we're told about the mechanism of natural selection is that if it got hard for the Irish elk to run through the forest, one would begin selecting out the Irish elk with shorter antlers and after a while, we'd have an Irish elk with short enough antlers to get along fine. We don't really understand the process of extinction.

BERRY: Individual extinction is an analog of racial or species extinction, isn't it? I mean, whatever it is that exists ceases to exist.

WALD: You mean death?

BERRY: Yes.

WALD: Natural death.

BERRY: No, death by mistake, by error.

WALD: By accident.

BERRY: By error.

WALD: By screwing in a light bulb while standing in the tub.

BERRY: All right. I've seen squirrels fall out of trees, and the reason that they don't fall out of trees more often is because they know they can and they're afraid they will, and so they make a judgment in favor of not falling out of trees.

WALD: Yes.

BERRY: And humans, it seems to me, are in the same fix. They can make errors too, with respect to what's outside. It's not all consciousness.

WALD: Yes, but, you know, we're a fine, vigorous species, if you wish, perhaps at the height of our potential, and if we wipe ourselves out now, that'll be a unique phenomenon in the history of the planet.

BERRY: Is knowledge what we're going to wipe ourselves out with, is that what you're saying?

WALD: I think it's a misuse of that knowledge, but damn little of it involves knowledge. It's greed, it's power, it's status, it's privilege. It's all those things.

ALLAN LEFCOWITZ: The implication would be that consciousness, possibly, is the mistake we make, considering the short time span, since it is the thing that gets us to talk after dinner, and to invent atomic bombs, and so forth. Is that, then, our biological mistake?

WALD: Well, I think that's in our mythology, the meaning of having eaten of the forbidden fruit. It means that we assume responsibility—we don't lay responsibility on animals, do we? Do we?

BERRY: They make mistakes, it's their fault.

WALD: Oh, yes, they make mistakes, but you wouldn't reproach them, would you?

BERRY: The nature of things reproaches them.

POURNELLE: It depends on the animal. You mean we don't say, "Bad dog"?

WALD: Yes, but there you're humanizing the animal and making him or her into a pet, into something convenient in your household. It's similar with your baby, too, you make your baby convenient not to wake you up in the middle of the night.

ROBERT SARGENT: I'd like to ask you something about your remarks about computers. Perhaps I interpreted you as not only attributing to a computer no consciousness but also as sort of barring consciousness forever from computers, but I was thinking that maybe if the human mind or if life's brain consists of molecules, material particles, or if computers are merely at a very rudimentary stage and if consciousness exists as a potential even in very elementary forms of life, would it then be possible that computers someday could have a consciousness?

WALD: You see, I think with the whole problem of consciousness, as I said, science can neither identify its presence nor its absence, and so we are left with a pure exercise of belief, of faith, or whatever you want to call it. See, I know that I see; I am glad to believe that all of you see. You're very much like me. Dogs, cats, pigs, cows are enough like me so I feel quite sure they see. There's nothing I can do to establish that belief that they react to light in ways that seem sensible, well, sure, but I can construct for you, with a little trouble, an electronic device that'll do that.

SARGENT: But if computers someday evolve?

WALD: Yes, so, you know, I was telling you, my own feeling is, yes, dogs, cats, cows, and so on see. I rather think that computers are not conscious, but there's nothing I can do about that either. So I'm just laying out my personal feeling. Yes, please.

POURNELLE: Hypothesize a biological as opposed to an electronic computer. What if I use some biological circuitry in it; now is it going to be conscious, are you going to allow it consciousness?

WALD: You know, it's like the question of What is life? Biologists, long ago, stopped defining life because any definition they made could be matched very quickly with some mechanical device. So they found it simply not useful to define life. I would include within that definition now (but you understand this is just my own attitude) being made out of the right materials, and those right materials are hydrogen, carbon, nitrogen, and oxygen. So I exclude—it's arbitrary, I agree, arbitrary—I exclude things made out of wires and tubes and so on.

SIR FRED HOYLE: I think there is a way by which one might understand consciousness, but only by taking a speculation that lies outside physics but otherwise within the realms of quite good physics. It's possible in physics to set up experiments in many ways where one or the other of two alternatives must happen; shall we say, either *A* or *Not A*. If this is done in a quantum mechanical system, a quite explicit result will come out: it will either be *A* or *Not A*. What the experiment defines is that, if he repeats his experiment under conditions which are judged, according to physics, to be identical, he doesn't get the same result each time. He sometimes gets *A* and he sometimes gets *Not A*. But it will be a definite sequence of *A*s and *Not A*s which you can read, if you please, as a sequence of dots and dashes. There will be a definite sequence, but this can in no way be predicted from inside physics. What can be predicted is the relative frequency of dots and dashes. And I suppose a physicist would say, if one examined one of these sequences, that it would be random. But I think there is no knowledge from inside physics that it has to be random. And so there is a means, if one cares to speculate, whereby one could have a message, an informational message in the dots and dashes. And then one could add the further speculation that our brains are of such a character, just due to their very nature, whereas a computer is not, that can actually read the system of dots and dashes and actually attach an information content to it.

One can make that speculation, and then one would have something that's not too far removed from decent physics.

WALD: Yes, this set of ideas I am working with has driven me into some strange questions. You know, if I make the sentence, "Consciousness is not the product, but the source, of the material universe," that sounds pretty wild. Though I could take you through "What have the major physicists said about the source of the material universe?" and you might be surprised. Not much better than that, but different in one regard, something which I will mention. If I make such a sentence, "Consciousness is the source of the material universe," you know, that sounds like a biologist trying to talk some physics, pretty strange. But if I make the sentence alternatively, "Matter in its essence, as far as one can go with it, is the solutions of the equations of quantum mechanics, quantum electrodynamics," that begins to sound like reasonable physics. That raises the question, "What are the solutions of those equations, and in fact what kind of thing is mathematics?" And some major physicists have asked exactly that question and discuss it no end, you know; how does it come about that there is something in that head-stuff? I think essentially those two statements are probably not very different from each other. What mathematics is, and mathematics certainly is something that we spin out of our heads—

BEALL: I think one can make an argument that the mathematics we might construct in our heads would be representative of the physical universe that we lived in. The laws of addition and subtraction are based on putting two stones together, going away and then finding two stones there. So it doesn't appear, at least to me, to be as obvious that pure mathematics is spun purely from imagination; I think it has a fairly good founding in reality. I think the fecundity of mathematics in physical systems is based on that founding in reality, but because it follows the structure of the brain—

WALD: But which came first, non-Euclidian geometry or the use found for it by rather recent physicists?

BEALL: But there was a non-Euclidian surface on the face of the earth even before non-Euclidian geometry was invented.

WALD: That's right, and—

BEALL: Telephone poles still converge to a point on the horizon, which is in essence a non-Euclidian space.

WALD: Yes, but you're picking awfully simple portions of mathematics. Mathematics is central to this meeting. A former colleague at Harvard, a Latinist, once spoke of Latin as representing in the humanities what mathematics does in the sciences. I think that is all wrong. I think what comes closest to the place of mathematics in the sciences is poetry. Poetry has enormous compression, spareness, exactness. A mathematician is a strange kind of poet in a way. And the mathematics that seemed a free play of the imagination was then found very useful by Einstein and physicists since. Now, I don't know whether you all realize how far out, in the popular sense, present physics is. Shocks me to death, because it was decided a while back (not so very long, but twenty years ago, perhaps more), to do away with the concept of forces such as unlike charges attracting each other and like charges repelling each other, like gravitation—for both of which one had perfectly simple formulas, you know: gravitation, the force as the product of the masses and divided by the square of the distance between them; and the same for electrical attractions, repulsions. Modern physics has decided, "No. No forces, these are all particle interactions." Forces would represent action at a distance; these are particle interactions. For example, the recent "Two bodies attract each other by gravitation," that's because they're exchanging gravitons. One hasn't found the gravitons, but one is looking for them, one assumes that they exist. Now, why do two electrons repel each other? Well, because each electron is surrounded by a cloud of, not real but virtual, photons. And the exchange of virtual photons is making the electrons shy apart from each other. Then I ask myself or any physicist who's handy, "What in God's name are you talking about?" We're making a whole physics, not only of real collisions but of virtual collisions. OK?

MacLEAN: You said, "What in God's name—" We missed that.

WALD: Yes, "What are you trying to say? What are you doing?" You know, that there are real collisions and virtual collisions. How does one have virtual collisions? Why aren't they observable? That's easy. The virtual collisions, it is said—this is the way one talks about them, the best physicists at present—the virtual collisions come inside of Heisenberg's uncertainty principle, so that they can't be observed and can't be measured because they fall inside of the limits of Heisenberg's uncertainty principle. Well, then I say, "Well, why do you go through a thing like this, you know, it's just a formalism," and I am told—Dick Feinman at Cal. Tech wrote the equation, and they come out with pretty much the right probabilities when you can solve them. So our criterion for reality has become the mathematics, and that makes one ask, "And what is mathematics?" We're far from your two stones.

WALTER JAMES MILLER: On my radio program, I once asked Gerald Feinberg, who I am sure you're familiar with, whether he expects that we're going to resolve Heisenberg's uncertainty principle, and he said, gravely, he expects that we'll find more uncertainty principles. I'd like to ask you a question that perhaps would be an analog in your field, based on your speech. You have talked about the eels' unity of response, and we are perhaps all nostalgic about that, those of us concerned with literature especially, because that's what literature is all about: the fact that we can't return to the eels' unity, you know. Do you see it possible that there will be a qualitative development in which we will reach, again, such a kind of unity, or that we will achieve a better interaction between consciousness and instinct, or is that the same thing?

WALD: I'm sure a lot of eels perish on this trip. Not all the eels come home. Oh, there must be untold loss, sure. But eels as the species don't make a mistake; they get home.

BERRY: Probably no American eels have gone to Europe . . . .

WALD: We have no report.

BRODERICK: Only when they die.

MILLER: Do you see a possibility of a qualitative development toward a higher unity, higher than the eels?

WALD: Yes, I do, and I have to write them out because they mean a lot to me. Because, you see, I think, I've been thinking a lot about children and what we do to them. You see, I play with the idea, I am taking great pleasure in these thoughts, so that's a sufficient excuse for having them, a great pleasure. I wonder about this one consciousness, a kind of universal consciousness. I haven't used the word *wisdom* in this talk yet, but it would be a wisdom, too. I think that—I'm talking very freely and loosely now, I can't prove anything—that young children are connected up to begin with, that they hardly divide that strange thing, the dream life, from the waking life, that they're kind of in communication with that universe, and that we observe them really being, so to speak, both primitive artists and scientists, and then we, in the developed world, put them on a track, because when you're on a track you're going somewhere. There's even a schedule; you know, one knows where one is heading, and the whole of society gangs up on a kid to do that at a pretty early age. And, you know, I've been in innumerable conversations in which parents say, "Oh, yes, they make such interesting paintings, but then it all stops when they're about ten." It is stopped, yes, and they're told, incidentally, at about that time, "It's time to stop playing and learn how to work." Right? Now, I must say, as a mature, over-mature, scientist, and I'm sure this is true equally—more so—in the arts, when the playing stops, there's nothing left but hacking. The playing is, in fact, the creative part of all human enterprises, and when the playing stops, there isn't a hell of a lot left that we find of interest. So I wonder whether the reality isn't that, yes, indeed, kids are put on a track, Einstein is brought to the point at which he starts working for the customs, and then, late in life, a few human beings work desperately to find their way back, with more or less success. Gee, I'm taking liberties with you, and I've already talked too much. I have a young daughter whom I love dearly, she's twenty. When she was nine and my son eleven, they were playing in her room. My son picked up a piece of paper, took a look at it, said, "This is a pretty good poem, Debbie," and showed it to my wife. Otherwise, it would have just gone out with the trash; it wasn't written for anyone; she wrote it. I am about to recite it to you. Why? Well, because I just can't imagine where that poem came from. And she resented the fact for a long time, she knew that I thought there would not be another. And, indeed, there was not another. By now she's stopped resenting it. Now, this is a nine-year-old, middle-class kid, private school, you know; kept in the house most of the time because it's dangerous for little girls to walk around the streets of Cambridge; so I'll tell you the poem.

If you ever get to infinity,
you will find me there,
for tomorrow I will climb
the elementary stair.
I will climb to the very top,
open up the door,
and look at all the ages
lying on the floor.

It never happened again, but where did it come from? Psychic communication?

ROBERT SOKOLOWSKI: You have pointed at consciousness from many different directions, and done so very effectively, but do you think there's a way of thinking about it to shed light on what it is? And I don't mean to go into the physiology behind it, but to talk about it in itself. Are there structures, patterns, repetitions, other parts that are worth bringing to mind?

WALD: Yes. One of the things that most comforts me in life is the realization that whenever and wherever, through the ages, in all kinds of cultures, someone has plunged deeply to ask that kind of question. They don't come out with the same answers, but they come out with strangely compatible answers, and that's an enormous comfort to me, I must say. I find when I read Lao-t'zu—in translation, of course, unfortunately—I feel Lao-t'zu closer to me than my colleagues at Harvard. I think that in the Eastern philosophies, mysticisms, consciousness is the source, not the product. It took me a day to realize that the sages have been saying that a long time, and their solution is a congruence of the smallest with the largest. The universality is built in, and the thought is that one has just a share in universal consciousness, which is Brahma, and Brahma dreams up a universe, and that's it. And then it lasts as long as he's awake, and then he goes into the night of Brahma, and it starts over again.

HOYLE: Do you regard Brahma to be inside the universe or outside the universe or identical with it? How do you interpret that?

WALD: What would you describe as outside the universe?

HOYLE: Well, in the sense in which I think the Judaic-Christian theology would have God, as outside the universe in the sense of an irreversible relation.

WALD: Yes. Well, but then, he's sitting on that little lotus throne in my heart, your heart, the heart of everybody here, if you're only willing to look at it that way. So, completely pervasive.

HOYLE: So it's almost an identity.

WALD: With the universe, yes, and hence the life and death cycle.

HOYLE: It's very interesting, because this is the intermediate between the Judaic-Christian, where God is greater than the universe, or the Greeks and the Norse, where the gods were less than the universe: in the Eastern one almost has an identity, which, in a way, looks more logical.

WALD: Yes, and which is all consciousness. And then, that is just the removal of the self, the *atman*, from one body to another. You occupy a body for a time, and then you seek out another.

STEPHEN S. BARATZ: Did those societies have the same ten-year-old shut-off thing as ours? The ten-year-old shut-off of the imagination in a child? Is that a product of us or do all societies share that, more or less?

WALD: I really don't know. You know, there has always been the possibility of that child. Sometimes the parent, in my reading, as it happens—no, not always a male, not always the male. But anyhow, the parent, being virtually a guru as well as a parent, but otherwise, the child can go to a sage, a guru, and begin to live that contemplative life as its life, as its whole life. I think these things have become, also, very degraded at this time. My own excursions, experiences with organized religion of every kind have proved very disappointing, and I have never had a real contact with a guru. That might be something very interesting; I just don't know.

MS. KUMIN: Could we take perhaps one more question and then adjourn, for you'll be besieged with other questions.

PHILIP APPLEMAN: Let me ask the question; it's too late for the answer, it's not too late for the question. Ninety-five percent or so of what we've been talking about this afternoon would be perfectly appropriate to a conference on science and philosophy. It is nothing very literary, so what I would have asked you earlier would have been to reflect a little on literature, and particularly such contemporary literature as you're interested in, and to ask you to reflect on specific examples of it insofar as how you, not as a literary critic but as a scientist, found these to be interesting or uninteresting, competent or incompetent, and so on. You may, if you want, give that thirty seconds now, but it's probably something we can talk about during the reception.

WALD: Well, I would like to say something about it, because science fiction is a very curious invention in literature. In the hands of a few people who write science fiction it is to be taken, I think, very seriously indeed. I was sent by one such person, Doris Lessing, to read Olaf Stapleton. Stapleton I found difficult to read, I was impatient with him, but Lessing, I think, is really trying to say something, and I was telling her about my problems with trying to express this consciousness-and-the-universe idea. She said, "Why don't you write it as science fiction? Because that gives you a freedom that *Science* magazine wouldn't permit you, you know, also space?" The other one whom I admire enormously but never met, Ursula Le Guin. I think she is to be taken very seriously; she is using her science fiction to hold a mirror up to human beings, to ask what kind of thing is a human being? How different could it be? How much better could it be? Also a mirror up to our society. So I think these are to be taken very seriously. In an entirely different vein, Faulkner is an author I read anything I could lay hands on, and reread.

MS. KUMIN: I think we could continue this during the reception, and I think we all join in thanking Dr. Wald for a lively afternoon.

SESSION 2
November 10, 1981

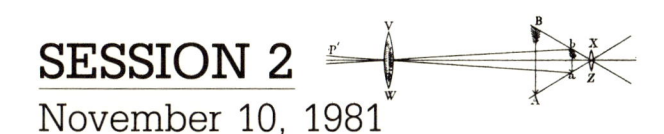

The Poetry of Nothing
O. B. HARDISON

Discussion
WILLIAM MEREDITH, Moderator

WILLIAM MEREDITH: I would like to say first that this conference is in a certain way a memorial to Robert Hayden, who, when he was here as Consultant, wanted to initiate this kind of an investigation. During the time that I was poetry consultant, we made some preliminary feints at this kind of gathering, which many of you took part in on one occasion. But as it stands now, this discussion is a memorial to the man who had an extraordinary grasp of humanity in the sense that Dr. Wald spoke of it yesterday. Robert Hayden was a scientist in the Renaissance sense, a man who understood what was happening to us in the twentieth century, and who manifested that particularly beautifully in a poem he did for the Bicentennial year, "An American Journal," in which the narrator is a man from another planet who has come to speak about us to his own people. We would like, I think, to acknowledge his seminal part in this conference, and Maxine Kumin, who has, of course, brought us here and is the present consultant, who will see it come to fruition today. As we start this morning, I would like to say I was bowled over by the presence of George Wald yesterday, and I think we assumed, somewhat, a classroom stance in asking questions of the speaker. We are all theoretically members of the conference and can make pronouncements looking straight ahead this morning, or ask questions of people that we find suspicious or interesting at the table, so that O. B. Hardison doesn't have to be schoolmaster for you, but he certainly has a lot to account for in this paper. O. B. Hardison.

O. B. HARDISON: I am very grateful to be here, grateful to the Library of Congress and to everybody who has had a part in this conference, because it's a subject that is fascinating to me and has become more and more fascinating over the years. My background is literature and literary criticism, and most of my work has been done in medieval and Renaissance studies, but I have found over the past few years that I have gotten more and more interested in what is happening in the twentieth century, and trying to get some way of using whatever skills I have developed in the course of my career in order to illuminate, at least for myself and maybe for other people, what seems to be happening. A conference on science and literature could go in a great many directions. You could talk about novels that have been written about scientists or about scientific investigations; you could even talk about thrillers that involve scientific secrets that have circulated around the world. Of course, you could talk about science fiction; I think that's a tremendously interesting topic. It's a topic which has been explored very extensively by a lot of writers, I think, in both the sciences and in the humanities. I'd say parenthetically that I think it's a topic that, curiously, really doesn't get to the heart of the questions that I see raised by the concurrence of the two words, science and literature. Somebody said yesterday that science fiction holds a mirror up to human nature, and I think that's right. And too often it holds a mirror up to human nature as it has been formed by traditional society and becomes either a comment on traditional society or a comment on ways that traditional society is being warped, frequently a satirical comment or a prophetic comment about the fact that science may be destroying certain things that are essential in human nature. I'd say that I don't think that science can destroy anything that's essential in human nature. I think it's an expression of human nature, and it allows human nature to develop in new ways and very important ways, and we're on a path that's been marked out by science; there is no possible way that we can turn back from the point of view that I take in the humanities. I think anything can be a humanity. Wordsworth looked at the natural scenery of England and all of a sudden that natural scenery was a humanity to him. The Hudson River school of painters looked at the grandeur of the Rocky Mountains or the pastoral beauty of the Hudson River area, and those things were humanities to them; they were talking about the human significance of these experiences. Well, you can find human significance in anything at all. In another mood, Wordsworth stood on Westminster Bridge and looked at London, and he said, "The earth hath not anything to show more fair; dull would he be of soul who could pass by a sight so touching in its majesty." You can look at death, you can look at things that are ugly, and you could still find human significance in them. In *King Lear*, we have an episode where a character is blinded on stage; his eyes are gouged out, and the blood runs down his face and so on, and yet, in a sense, there is a kind of terrible beauty in *King Lear*, which is grander than the beauty that you find even in a play like *Hamlet*. So I think anything can be a humanity, and taking that point of view, looking around me in the middle of the twentieth century, it seems to me that the most neglected of all the humanities in the twentieth century is the one that is most important in shaping our consciousness today, namely, science. And I have been trying to take a point of view toward science, drawing upon my background, which would enable me to talk in meaningful ways about its human significance. Since I am a literary person, I find that I can gain points of entry into this topic most readily from written material, though I think you can also gain points of entry from the visual arts and from a variety of other directions.

I started out trying to do a book on identity in technological society, and I faced the problem of how can you write about this kind of a topic, and specifically, how can you write about it if you are not going to write about it in terms of hard-edge science? My own scientific credentials stop with integral calculus, and while I did take a course in thermodynamics once, I parted company when they got to Maxwell's equations, which use partial differentials, and that was a little beyond me. So you could say I make no pretense whatsoever to be a scientist.

The strategy that I eventually chose was to begin with three written passages by three very interesting figures in the relatively recent history of science: a passage from Darwin's *Origin of Species;* a passage from a remarkable book which I'm sure many of you know, which has been influential in architecture and design as well as in science—maybe more so in architecture and design than in biology—namely D'Arcy Thompson's book on growth and form; and finally, ending up with a passage which I excerpted from an article by the physicist Yoichiro Nambu on particle physics, supplemented by some material by Murray Gell-Mann, who invented the word *quark* and derived it, as many of you know, from *Finnegans Wake* by James Joyce; and also about Werner Heisenberg, who wrote a sentence that correlates to a very beautiful sentence that Mr. Wald used yesterday in his talk. He said something to the effect that nature is the solution to the equations of quantum mechanics. And Heisenberg, in an essay on the image of nature in modern physics, says, "The farther we penetrate into nature, the more we catch glimpses of the image of the human face." And I think both of those statements are moving in somewhat the same direction.

So I began by trying to treat these three passages as I

SESSION 2

would treat a poem or a passage from a novel, using the techniques of close reading, trying to understand what the implications were of the literary style, the imagery, and so on. The passage I selected from Darwin is in the section on natural selection. It's a very famous and rather flowery passage in which he describes natural selection as producing what he calls a "tree of life." He is using a mythic image there, obviously parallel to the image in Genesis, but parallel to a great many other images as well, surprisingly literary for Darwin, who in his autobiography apologizes for having a lousy literary style. Apparently Darwin was very sensitive to the fact that he could not write flowery prose like Ruskin, although, I think, if read from the perspective of the twentieth century, he turns out to be a much better stylist than Ruskin—that being a sad comment on the way that literary fashion can turn an author almost against himself. But, at any rate, in this passage, Darwin describes the way that species occur. They produce branches on the tree of life, then many of these branches die. The tree grows, there are branches farther up on the tree of life. Sometimes a branch low on the tree of life will survive and put out leaves near the top of the tree of life, and then, he says, at the bottom of the tree, there is this infinite area covered with the bones of the generations that did not survive, with the price that was paid for having the tree there in the first place.

Well, there are lots of significant implications to that, beyond the fact that this is a mythic and religious image. Among the implications are those suggested by the very concept of height itself; height is good, depth is bad. The bones are at the bottom; the sun and the leaves are at the top. And that correlates, I think, to what a great many Victorians, beginning with Huxley, found in that evolution. What I think may be [implied]—with somewhat nervous apologies to Mr. Appleman, who is the expert on Darwin here—but I think (maybe it's clearly implied in Darwin as well) that evolution is a teleological process. Things get better as they get higher, and the more complex the organism, somehow, the better it is. And this process, which begins with single-celled organisms, culminates in the great blossom known as homo sapiens. I don't see any reason whatsoever in Darwin's basic concepts to believe that this is the case, but I think the interpretation of these concepts is saturated with values, and they are values which are very anthropocentric and which equate goodness with complex modes of intelligence and man on the evolutionary chain. Then the reference to the bones at the bottom is a very bitter and tragic concept, and again, Darwin is introducing human emotion into his equation. There's no reason to suppose that the amoeba laments its passing, or that the frog or the cockroach laments its passing. It just happens. These forms appear and they die, and they are replaced by other forms. But when Darwin looks at it, he makes it into a grand, tragic spectacle touched with this kind of almost divine, awesome beauty created by the fact that out of this tragedy grows the tree of life.

You move to D'Arcy Thompson, and you get a totally different view. D'Arcy Thompson claims to be the first person who systematically applies mathematics (particularly mathematical geometry) to the study of biological forms. I think people had done it before D'Arcy Thompson, but D'Arcy Thompson attempted to do it comprehensively. I don't know where D'Arcy Thompson stands among the biologists today, but his book is a brilliant adventure in the study of comparative morphology, the study of the way that forms can change while preserving certain geometrical relations. Curiously enough, D'Arcy Thompson is anti-Darwinian; he is opposed to Darwin. And that's because of the perspective he takes—a geometric and mathematical perspective rather than an anthropomorphic perspective. His mathematics is a cool way of looking at the world in contrast to a sort of anthropomorphic and tragic vision that you find in Darwin. He says that there is no particular reason to believe that a sparrow, for example, is better than a pterodactyl. They both flapped through the skies and presumably were quite successful in the periods in which they lived and to which they were adapted. But at a deeper level, he says if you understand life in terms of mathematical form, there's no such thing as evolution because mathematical form is eternal. A circle doesn't evolve; a sphere doesn't evolve. The principles required for close packing of cells do not evolve; they are mathematical principles, not principles related to something that changes over time. You can discover more of the mathematics if you are a mathematician, but we're not talking about evolution there, we're just talking about better understanding of a particular field. At the end of *On Growth and Form*, D'Arcy

Thompson steps back and contemplates what he has achieved, and he is awed by it. He quotes Genesis and John Milton, and he quotes other solemn passages about the awesome beauty of creation seen in terms of mathematics, its regularity, its conformity to these mathematical principles; and you realize, when you read that concluding passage, that there is a recurrence in D'Arcy Thompson of a motif that you find at the very beginning of *Science in the Western World*. He's a Pythagorean; he believes in the divine nature of numbers and the divine nature of the forms that are produced by these numbers, but by the same token—there's great beauty there—there's something missing from his equation which was in Darwin. It is the element of tragedy. D'Arcy Thompson's view is cool; the creator has made all things in number and proportion, and that is a magnificent thing to contemplate, but there's no tragedy in it. And since there's no tragedy, there is also no triumph, there is no tree of life moving up to the sunlight. It's a much more detached vision of life than you find in Darwin. Then I came to Yoichiro Nambu and I chose his work because, first off, it typified an element that I find indigenous in logic, at least since Lewis Carroll. An enormously playful element. You can find it today in the work of a most remarkable logician who also is a magician. He used to make his living by being a magician; his name is Raymond Smullyan, and he's got a whole book of logical problems that eventually leads up to an explication of Gödel's theorem, but it's all based upon the plot of *Alice in Wonderland* and Tweedledum and Tweedledee, and then you have a false Tweedledum and a false Tweedledee, but there's a playfulness about that, and that touches on a theme that was mentioned yesterday—again, I think very appropriately—the fact that there's a tremendously important element of play in science. Play is a kind of freedom, and that element of play in all creative activity (and I would claim it for art as well as science) is obvious in the work of somebody like Miró, an artist; it's obvious to me in the endless wordplay that you find in Shakespeare, his fascination with those egregious puns, the fact that he will stop the play when he's about to assassinate the king in *Macbeth*—he'll stop the play so the drunken porter can urinate on the castle courtyard. I think there's an enormous amount of play in all creative activity. I would remind you that that has been examined in relation to a very sophisticated philosophy of consciousness, and the person who, to me, did the definitive work is Schiller, the friend of Goethe and the poet, in a work called *Letters on the Aesthetic Education of Man*. Schiller identifies this key element in his system, he calls it the *spielsruhe*, the play impulse. And what I found in Nambu was a style that reflected that he was obviously having an enormous amount of fun talking about the eight-fold way of elementary particles and developing marvelous metaphors to describe the nature of quarks, of which he said that a quark is something of which the demonstration that it exists includes the demonstration that you cannot ever observe it. I don't know whether that's still true, but I found it a nice paradox; if you can prove it exists, you have simultaneously proved that you can never observe it. And he talks about quarks being enclosed in bags that can't be opened and tied upon strings that cannot be broken. Beyond that, I think what he is saying is something very close to what Dr. Wald said yesterday, nature is whatever we are able to conceive it to be at a given moment, and what has dropped out of Nambu is any notion of absolutes. Darwin has the anthropomorphic absolute, D'Arcy Thompson has the mathematical-Pythagorean absolute; for Nambu, nature is a series of what Wallace Stevens described as "necessary fictions." They are fictions because we know they are going to be replaced; they are necessary because we cannot get along without them. The mind is a machine that creates order, and whether the order is a mythical order or a religious order or a mathematical order, or whether the mind draws on a great many different orders at the same time, still a machine, still grinding out an order and it can't stop short of dying. What I think I found in Nambu was a statement that physics, science in general, has begun to elevate to the level of conscious principle that idea. I think it's always been implicit in science. If you say that science works with hypotheses, you're saying that science never claims to give absolute truth. You're saying that science is offering theories about the truth which are most useful in that they provide a basis for their own refutation, correction, improvement, and eventual replacement by another set of hypotheses. But Nambu was like a poet; he was just glorying in his literary style, in this playfulness which, as I say, I also find in writers like Lewis Carroll and Raymond Smullyan, and I find it also evident in the fact that Murray Gell-Mann would select the name of an elementary particle, quark, which is a funny word all by itself, from one of the strangest novels written in the twentieth century. And what I see from the curve that I have drawn there is a movement of human consciousness away from absolutes toward a situation where everything is recognized by it as provisional. And I think it's a very important development, maybe even evolutionary development in consciousness, and I think it has occurred within the last century. I think we're still in a world which is filled with enormous areas of cultural lag. A lot of people don't know quite yet what is happening to them, or has happened to them, but nonetheless I think it has happened.

Then, having done that, I wanted to take a look at what evidence there is that these concepts have impinged on consciousness and have reshaped consciousness. And that led me to the period roughly between 1895 and 1910, which is a period of explosive and fundamental new expression in a variety of areas. One of these areas is obviously science, physics in particular. People who talk about changes of attitude in the twentieth century sometimes mention Sigmund Freud, but I really don't think Freud gives us a new vision of man. I would say that, as I read Freud, it's an eighteenth-century association psychology written in a much more sophisticated and medically useful way. It seemed to many people to be a fundamentally new view of man, but I don't think it was. But I do think we get a new view of nature in the sequence of scientific theories that, so far as I understand them, extend, say, from Maxwell and Rutherford through Einstein and Bohr to Schrödinger and Dirac and Heisenberg and all those other giants of whom Dr. Wald spoke so eloquently yesterday. So that's happening in the world of physics, and if nature is changing, the mind is always sort of reciprocal to nature; the mind can change nature; you change the quantum equations, you've changed nature. But nature also, once having been shaped, forms a culture that surrounds us and that helps to shape the minds of children as they grow up. So nature changes the mind, always a two-way street there. But I found also that there were equally explosive and fundamental changes in the visual arts; I won't say I found this, because I guess all of us knew it, but all of a sudden, I found that I could use that information in a way I hadn't been able to use it before. And I suppose the development of cubism would be my sort of symbolic statement of that change. A radically new language; a language posited on the basis that all of the languages of the past that had come from tradition were no longer valid, that some new departure was near. And then, in the field of literature, there were also radical changes. We all know about James Joyce, we all know about Gertrude Stein, we all know about André Gide and Valéry, Thomas Mann, some of the great giants that are regularly taught in our courses in modernism, and I think there are tremendously useful things to be learned by studying these authors. And yet these authors don't seem to me to face up to the immensity of the change, and some of the authors who are described as being part of the modernist movement, like T. S. Eliot, for example, are really lamenting the passing of the old ways rather than trying to confront the new ways and create, forge a language adequate to express the new culture that is emerging.

Now, in doing this, I confronted a really strange paradox. In art—visual art and, to a lesser extent, in music—the new languages of the twentieth century seemed to be adapted easily, or relatively easily, and to be able to achieve widespread currency. As you all know, various kinds of abstraction, when they were first introduced, were greeted by outrage, and people would say, "A child could have done this or that"—probably an expression of praise, if rightly understood, and back to Professor Wald's point yesterday—but the critics gradually shut up as this new art made its way, and eventually the laments of the critics were replaced by the quiet scramble of the art investors at the auctions. All of a sudden, this art was worth a lot of money, and there's nothing in a materialistic society that succeeds like money. Language doesn't seem to be as adaptable to new modes of expression as art. And this gets into the question of science and literature. I think you'd have to say that language is an inherently conservative form. It is localized regionally, each language comes from a specific place on earth. It is complementary to a specific kind of culture, and it expresses that culture, and it is also, and maybe even most important of all, a kind of collective repository of history. Anybody who looks into a standard etymological dictionary is confronted with the archaeology of language instantly, and also confronted with its immense fascinations and the fascinating subterranean relationships there are between words that are apparently very different, and between words, even, and historical events, and lone words which reflect periods when cultures were in contact with each other. And language is what we inherit as we first develop consciousness as children; so as we become conscious, we have already internalized the history of our culture and our race, in these terms at least.

So language tells what everybody has done in the past, and its forms are adjusted so you can think thoughts that people have thought in the past, but suppose you confront a situation where the past is no longer relevant, where there's a new situation. There is nothing in language that can adequately cope with this problem. Hence you get the complaints, over and over again, particularly since the Romantic period, of the fact that when a poet tries to write, he or she is overwhelmed with stereotyped rhythms, with stereotyped images, with stereotyped verse forms, with stereotyped genres, everything you tend to produce begins to threaten to be a cliché. It's great in a traditional culture. Remember Alexander Pope said that the best art was "What oft was thought, but ne'er so well express'd." But what if you don't want to express "what oft was thought," but you want to have a new thought. So that's an enormous problem, and artists in the language have tried to confront it, and one of the devices they have used is a series of systematic distortions of normal language. If you can break up normal syntax and normal grammar, which are probably controlling your thinking at a much deeper level than the words themselves, if you can break them up by some type of systematic distortion or even a random distortion, is it possible that the words will fall out in a new way and you will be able to think truly new thoughts?

I chose in my paper, which has been distributed, three examples of efforts in that direction. First, dada, with its high priest, Tristian Tzara, and also his acolyte and perhaps an even greater figure in the movement, the magnificent Kurt Schwitters, the author of the sound sonata and the one-letter poem: dada, with its fascination with randomness. The dada poets liked to clip words from a journal, stir them up in a hat, and paste them down on a piece of paper in whatever order they came out, and I gave you a couple of examples of poems like that in the paper.

Second, I chose what is called concrete poetry, based on the notion that the word is dead in the sense of being no longer adequate to express modern experience, and on attempts to reshape language either so that the words come alive again (which, I think, is maybe a false direction) or in such a way that the words express their meaning visually almost in the manner of Chinese ideographs. [Thus] you get a transparent language, a language which is not parochial in the sense of being bound with a specific culture but is at least potentially a truly universal language, accessible to all people in the same way that visual art and music are accessible, or more or less accessible, to all people regardless of what language they may have learned when they grew up.

And finally, the last example I gave you was the poetry of Oulipo, which I describe as algorithmic poetry. That, in a sense, is the opposite of randomness; as a matter of fact, Georges Perec points out that Oulipo poets are highly systematic rather than random. What he doesn't point out is that applying a systematic formula which has nothing to do with grammar or syntax to language is pretty much the same thing as mixing up the words in a hat and pasting them on the page, because it produces a language different from the language that we've been used to speaking and, consequently, possibly a new language.

Well, having done that, I confronted two facts. One, most of this stuff looks pretty silly when you stand back and examine it. Maybe that's not a criticism; maybe there's an element of play there that is very important and expressive of the freedom of the human spirit. But at a deeper level, it seemed to me that this poetry was in some cases imitating things and in other cases anticipating things. It seems to me, obviously, the business of cutting the words out and pasting them on the page does the same thing to the esthetic of the newspaper that Brancusi did to the esthetic of the airplane propeller. Brancusi looks at a highly-finished mathematical surface, which is normally considered utilitarian, and he says, "There's a great esthetic there," but nobody notices it because you look at an airplane propeller and you say it's to make the plane fly, period. But it's there. So he abstracts the esthetic of a highly-finished curve, expresses it in a highly-finished chromium and steel piece of sculpture that has no use whatsoever, and you have to see it then because it only exists to be seen, it doesn't exist to get an airplane into the sky.

By the same token, there is an esthetic in the newspaper. It's a very strange esthetic if you try to formulate it. It's a random and discontinuous esthetic. You know what a book is. You get *War and Peace* off the shelf, there it is, you know it's a novel, you know it's by one person, you know more or less what it's about, Napoleon and Russia, and you start reading, and you go continuously from beginning to middle to end in a good Aristotelian fashion. But you take a newspaper and the first thing you do is you see the front page, it's a random collection of things, the only relation to each other being that they all happened within the same twenty-four hour period, and then they're sprinkled across the front page. Moreover, if you read the paper like I do, you never finish anything. I read the front page and I read half of an article about the AWACS sale, and it may end in mid-sentence, and that doesn't bother me. I go over to the next article, which is about the latest sexual scandal in Washington. I read that with great interest. My eye is stopped by a photograph of President Reagan smiling at a baby, then I go on to something about the Tombigbee Canal down in Tennessee and the latest rip-off of the taxpayer, and so on. And I finish all the front page first, and then I turn to the second page and I get some new articles, but then I also pick up second halves of some of the articles I have read and so on. But by the time I get to the third and fourth page, a new element has entered the picture, namely, all those advertisements for toothpaste and deodorants and things like that that are all sprinkled in amongst all these stories. That's a bizarre, discontinuous, perhaps highly playful but certainly a non-Aristotelian, kind of experience compared to the standard book of the nineteenth century or even of the twentieth century. So it may be that the dada people were trying to abstract the same aspect of the esthetic of what you would call "media art"—technically, art created by technology—and sort of identify it so they could objectify it, see what it was and respond to it. That discontinuous nature seems to me to run through all media art. Could you imagine anything more incredibly dada than a television program: in the example I used in the paper, your hero is dying in the cancer ward, he's a terminal case, his girlfriend is there, she's got her arm around his neck, she's about to kiss him one last farewell kiss before he goes over the top, cut. All of a sudden, you get a Kotex advertisement, an advertisement for Datsun, "We are driven," a station break, a little excerpt from the evening news, a couple more advertisements, for Schick injector razors, then cut, back to the cancer ward and the dying kiss. And that forms an hour block, and I say it's all part of the same experience. We pretend, to ourselves, that we turn our minds off during the commercials and we only watch the play; but in fact, we're watching the whole thing, and that esthetic is a bizarre, again, slightly random esthetic.

I tried to find other examples of the way in which this kind of art is significant, and this Sunday I had a magnificent example of the relevance of the art of concrete poets. They are normally considered to be a rather esoteric and limited group of writers in the sense that they are trying to abstract an esthetic from a use and call attention to it. It's concrete poetry that drives Madison Avenue, and here's a magnificent article from *Potomac* magazine this Sunday on the art of cigarette packages, discussing the enormous amount of time and effort and money that goes into these things, the effort being to take a word, or a couple of words, like "Virginia Slims," identify this visually, and make it universal, so even somebody who is illiterate will know that's a package of Virginia Slims. And one of the fascinating things is the more you get into this, the more you begin to see, particularly with the Virginia Slims package, a close relationship between the esthetic of the cigarette package and the esthetic of the Bauhaus. There's an obvious relationship between this cigarette package, which is a tall rectangular solid, and the esthetic of the U.N. building in New York City, also a tall, rectangular solid with very strong verticals and horizontals, and great emphasis on right angles. So maybe these poets are not so dumb, maybe they're saying something that's worth listening to.

MEREDITH: It occurred to me that the literary examples given were so carefully chosen that we probably ought, some of us who are writers, to address ourselves to them and possibly say why none, to my knowledge, of the poets at the table have engaged in this kind of experiment and probably have been, as I was, rather surprised at the intellectual consistency and the intellectual pigheadedness with which it's been pursued by serious artists in the twentieth century. I think I put it out of my mind originally, having studied Apollinaire and having studied it as a historical event of the second decade of the century, so that when it was brought up again by people who might not have known that they were repeating history—I think of Richard Kostelanetz—concrete poetry didn't seem to me to be so much avant garde as a place that we'd traveled to and come back from. I'd like to, for the moment, ask for literary comments on this and, possibly, the literary comments suggesting how, as O. B. has demonstrated, these are really products of technological inquiry as much as esthetic.

BERRY: I'd like to ask what are the critical standards of this sort of writing, of art? You've offered only one, commercial success.

HARDISON: I think the art itself, concrete poetry, has had miniscule commercial success. I am saying that the concrete poets seem to be, let's say, complementary to a kind of art which is done with an entirely different and very utilitarian consciousness of what is being achieved and as much indifference to the esthetic result as perhaps the designer of the airplane propeller has to whether it's a pretty thing or not. He wants it to pull the airplane.

MEREDITH: To answer your question, one of the things that they insist on as part of their freedom is not only freedom from the conventions of the past but from the critical conventions of the past, so that you can't judge them except by the terms that they set.

BERRY: All right, then another point of clarification. In order to make sense of this kind of work, then, don't you have to dissociate yourself completely from the values conventionally attributed to words like *free, liberation, conservatism,* and so on?

MEREDITH: I would think they would feel that was a little bit nineteenth-century in attitude; yes, I think they have liberated themselves.

BERRY: Dr. Hardison is using those words at their traditional face value.

HARDISON: I think I'm probably using the term *free* in its Kantian sense, in the sense of somehow escaping from the determinism of the association of ideas, whatever variation upon association of ideas you would want to introduce.

BERRY: Well, that's a conventional definition.

HARDISON: I'm not sure the Kantian definition is a conventional one, but if it is conventional, so be it.

BERRY: Well, it comes out of the past.

HARDISON: It does, certainly.

PRAMOD LAD: Would you say that if you took a particular word, say *science*, and put it on a page and wrote it in a number of different configurations, that you would have all the connections from the past that that word has gathered?

HARDISON: No, if you read my paper you will see that I point out that there is a fundamental contradiction between the fact that these people use natural languages, which are vehicles of the meaning of the past, and that they want to achieve what I call *transparency*, that is, accessibility beyond a particular cultural and parochial area. Logically speaking, I say in my paper, the only perfectly transparent language would be one using a phonetic system that had never been used before and, if it's written, it's written in an alphabet that has never been used before. As a matter of fact, there have been experiments in computer generation of bizarre alphabets, but it would be a language which would be transparent only because it was equally unintelligible to every human being. So there is a paradox, and you can see this very clearly in the concrete poets, who will talk about their desire to achieve a universal language and their desire to achieve freedom from the dead and deadening traditions of the past, but who very frequently turn out to use their language in quite traditional, romantic ways as a way of emphasizing the traditional meanings of words rather than escaping from them. I've provided a good many examples in the illustrations attached to that paper, and Gomringer is a perfect example. Gomringer started his literary career writing in German, but he was born, I think, in Bolivia, and so when he became a concrete poet he reverted to Spanish, which is illogical. If you're going to be truly universal, it suggests a sense of traditionalism, of attachment to a culture and a tradition, and in his poems—I gave one called "avenidas y mujeres"; it is a very simple poem—you might describe it as a minimalist lyric, but it's still very recognizably a lyric in the Romantic tradition. There's another poem he wrote, "silencio," which does just what you say; he tries to arrange the word *silence* in such a manner that the marvelous thing is, there's a big hole right in the middle of the poem; that's the silence. But that hole expresses the meaning of the word, the lexical meaning of the word, so it is not a way of escaping from the traditional meaning, it's a way of making the traditional meaning of the word more immediate, of reviving its traditional value.

LAD: The thing that sort of puzzled me is the fact that these are experiments in which the failure of these experiments seems to be built into the enterprise, and that distinguishes it from a scientific experiment. So, for example, with the dadaists, there is a sequence of random words picked out of a hat, which may not, or need not, generate any sense; or the concrete poetry, the connections of words which have to be broken in order to restore the word; and, as far as the algorhythmic poetry is concerned, there is a sequence to it, but the sequence need not generate any sense. So these are all experiments which are sort of quests for failures, and a scientist constructing an experiment would not, I think, set about it in terms which are so severely contradictory that the very act of carrying out the experiment would almost instantly insure, in the case of some important senses, its failure.

HARDISON: Well, we're talking about a cultural form, I think, rather than a scientific experiment in your sense of the term. I will say that one of the objects of art—and I try to talk about that in the introduction of the paper—is to help us see and understand the world we live in. And here we are, we're talking about dada, we are examining aspects of the world as extensive as contemporary architecture and advertising and the esthetic of the daily newspaper which shapes our consciousness very profoundly, so I would say that's a demonstration of the success of the experiment.

LEFCOWITZ: I'm wondering if a good deal of this art wasn't based on a fallacious assumption about science. Possibly because they reacted to science, many of these artists reacted to science without understanding at least the mechanisms of science. We have this post-modern disappointment in the adequacy of language, I think, based on maybe false analogy to indeterminacy, and, on one level, language is always adequate even to express its inadequacy, and I'm wondering, if you look at Kostelanetz's poems—

HARDISON: I would disagree with that. Let me say that the motif of writer's block, of silence, has been a very important motif in modern literature, and I introduced it in this paper with Mallarmé. He was constantly being baffled by the fact that he had a great urge to express himself, but somehow or other the language wasn't adequate, and that poem, "Un Coup de Dés," is fascinating, maybe the greatest. In fact, a whole volume of poetics has been written by a French critic just on that single poem. It enacts the struggle of the poet to forge a new language to overcome silence, and the page itself, it has characteristics of the concrete poem, the blank page is the blankness of the chaos that surrounds us; it is also, since the poem uses the image of a sea journey, it is also, the blank page is an image of the sea, the words are the order being imposed on the chaos by the mind as it throws the dice. To go up to a much more recent example, Bucky Fuller says that at about age forty, he became totally dissatisfied with the language that was available to him, and so for ten years he essentially stopped talking. When he started again, he started talking in Fullerese, which, as many of you know, is a kind of a bizarre language. But it's a fascinating thing, it's the motif of silence once again.

LEFCOWITZ: I'm wondering if you start with a concept that's framed in the natural language, even the concept of the inadequacy of the natural language, and then they try to translate it, in some examples, as I looked at them, into this non-language, opaque language, random language, and then, in a way, expect the naive viewer to translate it back into the natural language, if you take a look at Kostelanetz's poem, for example. And so, to achieve the random effect, they achieve it through a method of translation from a natural, well, let me give you an example . . . you say, "That looks absurd." They say, "Precisely." So you've gone from their concept of, let's say, the absurdity of randomness of nature to an object randomly produced to a statement back into the natural language of absurdity. And I'm wondering if that isn't a misinterpretation, in part, of what the scientist is trying to do?

MILLER: I see a perfect parallel here. What O. B. is trying to say, says so well in the paper, is that literature lags here behind fine arts and science in that it's extremely difficult to get back to zero, and it's important to get back to zero. And when Descartes tries to do it and has the good luck of a three-day blizzard so that he can think away all preconceptions. I feel that if the blizzard had lasted four days, he would have scrapped even the one that was left. But one of the arts that O. B. is talking about is trying to do what Descartes was trying to do, to get back to a zero. And that is so natural in science, and yet, when we do it in the arts, it's outrageous. And Hemingway does it when he's describing a formation getting decorations, and he says, "We had heard abstract words like glory and nobility so often that they had no meaning for us any more." Hemingway's generation tried to get back to it, Beckett does it, tries to get back to the zero, and you have said that so well in your paper that I think that your problem is, if I may take analogies from two fields, your problem is like the problem that McLuhan had and the problem that Newton had. Once we understood what McLuhan was saying and once Newton's peers understood what he was saying, there was nothing more to say. You have done that for our problem about getting back to zero.

RICHARD WARREN SELTZER, JR.: One thing occurs to me in your opening remarks about Darwin, etcetera. As I was hearing what you were saying about these kinds of poetry, I was sort of going through that evolution. And my first reaction to a kind of poetry that I can't make sense out of is, "Oh, my goodness, it's modern, it's the most recent thing, it's those leaves at the top of the tree," and I'm attaching a value judgment to it from that point of view. And then there's the other approach that you touched on when you mentioned that, well, this is something that happened early in the twentieth century, and it wasn't a particularly successful experiment, and now here are people trying to do it again. That gave me a feeling of the bones at the bottom of the tree and looking at it from that point of view. Then I saw the other aspect of it too, the notion of the forms. You know, here we are exploring a new form that somehow exists internally, but now people are seeing it, and it exists side-by-side with other forms of poetry or literature. But I think that the link that probably ties this whole thing together with science, and seems to be sort of the crux of the value of the thing, is that it seems to be an experiment, this poetry, a sort of a demonstration of the mind's persistent need to see meaning anywhere. Like any experiment, it's most successful if you eliminate all the things that aren't concerned with that particular variable. So that the more random this thing is, the more precise an experiment it is of how hard the mind is really going to go to make sense out of that. What makes it striking is that the mind does persist that way, and also what makes it very trivial, because you have been so narrowly focusing on it you're not dealing with anything having to do with human experience. There is some link of connection with science and scientific method, but, okay, so what? How do we talk about human experience? This is one small part of human experience, but it seems uncomfortable talking about it as somehow a classic example of literature and its link with science. It seems to leave so much out in the course of becoming an experiment.

HARDISON: If I can comment on that briefly, I think I am trying to raise a question here, and the question is whether this little *Blick ins Chaos,* this little opening that emerges at the beginning of the twentieth century, isn't a much more accurate image of what is a true human experience in an increasingly technological world than all these nice sentimental romantic poems which keep telling us the world hasn't changed, things are the same, "this will go on though dynasties pass," to quote Thomas Hardy. I think dynasties have passed. Now, I think that there is a big problem in language. It is, as I've said before, tradition. But, somehow or other—one of the things that I was hoping would be discussed, because I'd like to hear the conclusions—somehow or other art doesn't seem to have this problem. Abstraction is accepted. It's so fully accepted that right now it may be even slightly passé. And we're getting superrealism today, which I think is another fascinating development in art. But it's a part of our experience, and it certainly is not trivial; certainly it reflects an aspect of twentieth-century experience. I think it reflects a changing nature of human identity. In music I suppose the most obvious practitioner of randomness on a conscious basis is John Cage, who has recently given up the I'Ching in writing his aleatory compositions, and he has gotten a computer to turn out lists of random numbers to help him achieve true randomness. So I think the motifs that you find in this literature run very deep in twentieth-century art and consequently, I assume, in twentieth-century experience. Though I come back to the fact that we always dig our heels in when language is at issue because it is so intimate to us.

HOYLE: I once had a demonstration of this thirty years ago. The scene was Chicago, and I was invited out to dinner by an Italian who had become a professor of physics at the University of Chicago—it wasn't Enrico Fermi, as the rest of the story will show. He brought two of his associates, as he called them, who were Japanese. One spoke a little English and the other absolutely no English at all. So there were the four of us, and, as I discovered, the Italian had got me along there, trying to persuade me that a theory of his was correct, and it was a crazy theory. And because he was paying for the dinner, I had to be polite, and we had the Japanese who spoke a little English trying to translate to the Japanese who spoke no English. So, as you can see, we had the sort of situation that maybe the Ford Foundation would have spent a million dollars to set up. Anyway, the Japanese who spoke no English sat like a dark brooding figure in the corner, I thought he must be dreaming of the samurai or something of the sort. But after about an hour he sort of exploded like a volcano and, translating as best I can what he said via the intermediary, what he said was, "The old fellow is crazy," and—I was much younger at that time, so I knew it wasn't me—and then he proceeded to lay the problem out precisely as I had been trying to put it. And so I then realized that in what you call the inner part, the Japanese who spoke no English, he didn't know a syllable of English (and I didn't know a syllable of Japanese) had exactly the same inner part that I had myself, whereas the Italian, that I could communicate with easily, had a totally different inner part. So, as I see it, we each have these inner regions which have a quality of multidimensionality, and we seek to communicate with each other in various ways. The artist has the great advantage that I think he gets into this inner region kind of in one move, whereas the literary person has a more complicated process. But the advantage of the word is it will convey much more complicated messages. But I think we are only really successful in conveying a universal message if it is what I might call unidimensional. It just is like a tape recording. And those will go through very readily, of which perhaps the best example would be mathematics, because although mathematics may look like symbols, symbols are simply shorthand for blocks of words. But the essence of a mathematical argument is that it must be rigorously linear, and because it sticks to that linearity, it can achieve great complexity. A good-quality journalism would be an example of a pretty linear argument in the literary form, which instantly conveys its meaning. And it seems to me, when one gets to literature, and especially to poetry, what the writer is then trying to do is to express the true multidimensionality of that inner region that you spoke of, but that it isn't usually successful—in fact, perhaps never successful—in the respect that the writer then has to give some grounds just as you're saying in your paper, in the sense of universality. The writing, then, becomes committed to the particular culture, and even to sub-elements in that culture, in order to achieve the multidimensionality. And it seems to me, when I read your paper, the problem you had addressed is how can you have your cake and eat it? How can you be multidimensional and yet be universal? And I think if I were a writer or a poet myself, I would really address this problem because, it seems to me, by giving away meaning, the problem isn't solved. I think that's what you're really saying, that it is a necessary failure, if one gives away meaning, but how to preserve meaning and yet have something that will go. I think if I were a poet, now, having read your paper, I would maybe set myself the problem of how to write a poem that could be fed into the computer which has the intercommunicating dictionaries to a number of other major languages, which have also the elements of the syntaxes of the various languages built into them, and to come out in the other languages as a poem that could have an esthetic meaning to other peoples. I think that might be quite an interesting project.

HARDISON: There have been a lot of experiments in computer poetry, and by and large, when you give a fairly simple formula, like the formula for haiku, the computer can do a pretty decent job. When you get more complex poetry, typically, with its combinations and permutations, the computer just combines the various elements—syntactical, grammatical, and lexical—in a thousand different ways and prints them out, and maybe out of those thousand different ways—

HOYLE: What happens in some of the passages in Shakespeare, if one has to compute it, translate it, say into Japanese, does it come out in a way, do you have to—

HARDISON: First off, I'm not aware of any efforts to translate

Shakespeare. I was talking about computer programs. I think, if I am not mistaken, and the scientists in this group can correct me, that there was a great effort on the part of the Department of Defense to develop machine translation, particularly from Chinese and Russian—

POURNELLE: The U.S. government was absolutely certain they were going to have machine translation within five years, and interestingly enough, everybody is still absolutely certain they're going to have it in five years. But it's been twenty-five years, and it's still going to be in five years.

HOYLE: It's the multidimensionality that's difficult to overcome.

HARDISON: I don't think machine translation is a viable concept at the present time. What it has demonstrated, I think very conclusively, is the opacity of natural language.

HOYLE: Yes, this is the challenge.

HARDISON: And this: they're facing the same problem that I would face if I translated, you know, a very simple poem by Goethe. I've tried to translate "Uber alle" for the last twenty years, and I've got many, many different translations, but none of them is Goethe.

SKLAREW: I'm thinking about four perfectly transparent images. The first, music, which has the kinds of configurations that restore and convey culture, okay? Then I'm thinking about mathematics, which I would say less conveys culture and is transparent. Then I'm thinking about acronyms and computer language. And the fourth and most fascinating, and maybe the best example, is the nucleic acid alternation on the DNA molecule, which, in a sense, does the best job of conveying the culture. That's its function. And there it is, a perfectly transparent language. We don't know how to read it, all of it, yet; but it clearly is, and the language in which the culture is conveyed is transparent and unattached to the culture. The language itself, it's mathematical.

POURNELLE: Do you notice what you've done here? You've given four examples, three of which have a common property, namely, that they have very precise rules. Mathematics; computer languages, which have extremely precise syntax, so much so that the confusion of a period with a semicolon will absolutely destroy your program; and DNA, which has enormous redundancy built into it, so that it doesn't have to have quite such a precise syntax, but still, it has very carefully constructed rules to it; and music, which has no rules at all, but and which—there's an equivalent to the dadaist movement in music where the random notes and so forth were attempted, and they say that's music too.

HARDISON: Mozart wrote that.

POURNELLE: Now, what did music have in common with the other three? I think I know exactly what you're trying to say, and while I can't understand what you've said, I'm sure there's something there. We have three things with very precise rules and one in which everybody keeps trying to say there are no rules at all, and yet you say they're all four transparent languages.

SKLAREW: Well, I would just like to say that my real question or concern is the development—we have no choice, these languages develop. But the concern is the conveyance of the culture, of what is valuable in the culture, or simply present, and I was just trying to find a model for a conveyance in which you can have everything, in which you can have the culture and the transparency.

BEALL: It occurs to me that we have made metaphors of our problem here, and one of the metaphors we have made is we've taken the physical world and the relationships in it and tried, metaphorically, through science, to talk about the physical world. That's what scientific laws are. That's what Newton's mechanics are, they're metaphors for the physical world. They're not the physical world. But we have moved from that metaphoric language to more and more abstract metaphoric language in science as we have gone into deeper and deeper understandings of the physical world. We then take, by parallel reasoning, which is very common in science, the idea that, since there is abstraction in science, we can interpret the abstraction in art in a parallel way, and that the movement away from physical representation is, in some sense, parallel, and therefore, deeper than the movement that one would expect if we were to stay representational with painting, for instance. We then try to apply that abstraction to literature, and, in doing that, what we first do is logically equivalent to taking away the painter's pigment, canvas, and brushes. That is, it seems to me that the real relationships in language are in effect the pigments that we use, the syntax and the grammar, and that by removing those, as the dadaist and the algorithmic poet would, we are in some sense constraining language a lot more than we expect contemporary paintings to be constrained or contemporary music to be constrained.

MS. KUMIN: That's a very good point. I think maybe the problem is semantic. We're calling these *experiments,* by a term that for centuries has been applied to cries from the heart distilled through imagery, that which we call poetry. And maybe we should just change the term. I don't think we can call these experiments poems; we can call them graphics of some sort. Because connotative meanings are going to linger as long as you're dealing in language; there's no way you can divorce meanings from words. There will always be these associative links; even if you just use an eye chart, it's very hard not to make associative links to the configurations that the ophthalmologist puts at the end of the room for you. And I think this is why the poets around this table are cringing a little before the label of poetry applied to what are essentially, I think, graphics.

LINDA PASTAN: To take this from a slightly more simplistic view and to address the question of why, perhaps, we are willing to accept this kind of experimentation in art and in music and—

HARDISON: Could I just beg one indulgence? I think every poem is an experiment.

PASTAN: Okay, but you do point out that we're willing to accept certain things in art and in music before we do in language, and I think that one of the reasons that that's true is that, what Maxine said about pigment, there's an immediate sensory pleasure in looking at some of these works of art that we're not necessarily understanding, in the color, and again, in the sound of the music. But when you're working with language, if you have divorced meaning and associations and become random enough, there isn't the sensory pleasure left to give us anything. I think that when we read very difficult and obscure poetry that takes an enormous amount of work to penetrate, we're willing to do this with poetry that, even though we're not understanding it, gives us a certain first-reading pleasure even though we don't know what we're reading. Students will be willing to work hard on understanding and looking up the literary antecedents of *The Wasteland,* because even when they're not understanding it they're getting something in the language and in the sound, whereas, in much of the dada stuff there isn't that genius behind it that has given that sensory pleasure first. Perhaps we're willing to work on Joyce because his language is so musical that we're getting a sensory pleasure from that. But one of the, perhaps, differences between science and art is that so much of both is to understand and to learn, but in art the element of pleasure is equally important, I think.

HARDISON: Well, let me say that I would go back to my little definition, which is the epigraph of my paper, by Barr, about art helping us see and understand. It seems to me that the pleasure is probably secondary to the seeing and the understanding, and sometimes the seeing and the understanding can be very painful. I would like, at least for my own purposes, to try to regard what these people are telling us as something which is perhaps painful, because it tells us something about the fact that we are going to have to leave home, we're going to have to change, and we don't want to do that, and consequently, we don't like to face up to the implications of what these works of art are saying. But if art forces us to acknowledge a truth, even though it is an unpleasant truth, it seems to me it's performing its function, and that the criteria of beauty and pleasure are probably secondary. Yeats talked about the raid on the Irish post office in 1916; "a terrible beauty is born." Rilke talks about "what is beauty but the beginning of terror that we can only barely endure" in his first Guignol elegy. If you take those things seriously, that's not very pretty, it's not very pleasant, but it is high art.

KARREN ALENIER: Don't you think, though, that the poetry of nothing, the ultimate goal of it, is to supersede language, that there is a desire to communicate beyond what is the limitation of perhaps what we capitalize as The Word? And that there is some desire to get to a very primitive level of consciousness, and that this is, in fact, a flirtation with the ultimate black hole, that this is another example of the desire of human beings to return, perhaps, to the zero, or it's a thrill, the thrill of going down and perhaps not going all the way down, but touching down and then maybe, if we're lucky, coming back up. But it leads to the second law of thermodynamics again, and we brought that question up yesterday, and isn't that what's being posited here?

HARDISON: I think certain kinds of this art do have that quality. I point out that the Eiffel Tower is frequently seen as a phallic symbol, that's primitive. I pointed out that Kurt Schwitters's "W" poem, which is described in the paper, seemed to certain people who heard it to have the quality of a primitive lament, and it seems to be related, obviously, to glossolalia, which is a fascinating concept. Other kinds of this art are very cool; they don't seem to have that primitive, connotative quality. They seem to point in exactly the opposite direction, toward, perhaps, what Dr. Wald was getting at when he talked about, well, what I derive from his talk about the one mind, a kind of globalization of consciousness, a new form of identity. I find Teilhard de Chardin talking about the same thing in *The Phenomenon of Man,* by the way. So I think some of it is primitive and some of it not.

BERRY: I confess that this meeting, like other meetings of the kind that I've been in, is beginning to frighten me, and what frightens me about it is the ability of gifted and highly educated people to carry on long conversations as if intellectual events were the only events and as if the world where these events have consequences and turn into other events were somehow far, far away. These conversations, these meetings, typically take place in windowless rooms. I'd like to interject something of that other world in order to say, as quickly as I can, what my own understanding of language is, because I can't speak of it at a theoretical level. What I want to interject is the problem of soil erosion, which is a cultural phenomenon and a scientific phenomenon; it's been caused both ways. It would be very hard to sort out the lineages of cause. Nevertheless, one of the new things in our situation is that we're eroding soil at unprecedented rates, and this implies several dangers. Iowa is spending, according to the U.S. Department of Agriculture, six bushels of topsoil for every bushel of corn that it produces; the state of Washington is spending twenty bushels of topsoil for every bushel of wheat. As far as I know, there's no proven new way, in all this age of innovation, to stop soil erosion, although there are several proven old ways to do it. But in order to stop it, on the scale at which it's being caused, it seems to me you have to have two kinds of language. One, you have to have a language to which I would attach the word *natural:* a strong, local language, that is, a language of direct reference to things and therefore capable of bearing minutely particular instructions about the management of parcels of land. Also, a language that can carry the load of moral instruction. You also have to have what I would call the distinction between low culture and high culture. You have to have, at the high culture level, what we would call—some of us, maybe—a literate language that's capable of coming at that same problem from a more general level, capable of making the connection between a particular place and every place, of formulating public attitudes. It seems to me that literature has always done exactly this sort of operation, made that connection at the level of language. It happened with Dante, it happened with Wordsworth, it happened with William Carlos Williams, it happened many times, where the literate language is carried back to meet the local, or the natural, language. And you must assume that there would be all kinds of instances where local speakers would carry down the literate, or the high-culture, or the intellectual language to meet the local or the natural language. And this is a cross-fertilization that's necessary for language to have any vitality and meaning at all. But also literature has always carried the capacity for revealing that grand and grandiose events are smally felt, and even at moments has had the capacity for revealing and insisting that grand accomplishments are smally done, in details by mostly anonymous individuals. So although I'm willing to acknowledge that there are things in intellectual life that are mind-blowing and all that, and that some new things are at hand, I would insist, too, that some old things are at hand. For instance, how do you conserve soil? How do you produce food? How do you build shelter? How do you make clothes? How do you get the buttons sewed on right? Those things are all questions of great worth, and I don't see how these independent trajectories, these unbraided trajectories of various cultural functions going off on their own and trying to be pure will ever speak to that situation. It seems to me that a language that wants to be pure and independent is exactly analogous to a science which wants to be pure and independent, which produces atomic warfare or economics; or an economy that wants to be pure and independent, which is bound to produce inflation, that is, money disconnected from chickens and shoes. Somehow it seems to me that the frontier, and the exciting one, is how to rebraid these strands, and that's what I had hoped this conference would talk about by getting these disparate disciplines into the same room. How do you bring cultural considerations to bear upon scientific activity? I think that's of urgent importance, and to me, always involved in it is the question of where lines shall be drawn. What, having these abilities and this knowledge, shall we do with it, and mustn't there be, I would ask, mustn't there be something that we won't do? I'm not much interested in getting out of the human definition myself, and so to me the question is inevitable, as I think it was to Macbeth, who said "I dare do all that may become a man; who dares do more is none." And when he dared do more, which he did, he didn't become more than a man, he became a hellish monster. That's probably my statement.

SOKOLOWSKI: In response to that, I think I'd agree with what you said, if I just may make a comment preliminary to my question to Mr. Hardison. It seems to me that one of the problems that leads to what you're talking about, and which also is assumed by the paper, is the idea of data as just there and then the mind putting all the order into it. It seems to me there is order in data to some extent, and that's much too radical a separation. It's really an epistemological point of view that's been with us for four or five hundred years. You find it in Hobbes, you find it in Locke, but it's just dead, it's just not valid or realistic, it's corrupt currency. And it seems to me the theoretical linkup that one might look to is to get rid of that notion of raw data coming in and then processed by a mind that puts all the order into it. Now, to say that the mind doesn't do anything would be foolish—obviously, there's some sort of back-and-forth operating here which has to be handled in a sophisticated way to account for the development of science—but I believe that that very deep starting point which you assume is the condition our minds are in is very much open to question. That really is in response to your comments, and I'd like to move to another point, which deals more with the literary work as an object on its own. And I wonder if you haven't exaggerated in saying that these processes that you find in these examples are all processes of subtraction. Isn't it a matter of using one lever to put pressure on another, to draw attention to something that hasn't been noticed, such as the page on which the work is written? When you do that, you really don't subtract, necessarily. What you do is use something else, a printed sign, to draw attention to the empty page. It defamiliarizes, to use that Russian formalist term, it defamiliarizes something you normally look through. So it seems to me there's much more of a positive achievement by many of these moves, both in the syntax and in the presentation of a poem; that is, by looking at things such as the background on which the thing is writen or the phonemic signs which are repeated and played with. You change meaning but keep that static, or you change that and keep the meaning static. Now, these back-and-forth processes bring out unusual relationships that are normally not noticed. And the reason they look grotesque is that we normally look through them. They're made to look grotesque so you'll look at them, but that's not a subtraction or an elimination. It's a positive move which gives you more resources to work with. Would you see that as different from what you've said?

HARDISON: No, I think that's not only a very perceptive point but one which is treated very interestingly in a lengthy discussion on figure and ground in Douglas Hofstadter's book *Gödel, Escher, Bach,* particularly in connection with the work of the artist M. C. Escher, who was fascinated with this problem but also with some fascinating examples where the ground becomes the figure in a written message. You have to look at it for a long time; it's like looking at a stick figure of a box, which, for a long time, seems to go into the page, and then you look at it again and all of a sudden it's sticking out of the page at you. You look at this figure in Hofstadter's book and all of a sudden—you've looked at it ten times before and you didn't get anything—bang, the message is staring at you. Yes, there are fascinating modes of expressiveness to be achieved in that way, and I think it's obvious in this cigarette-package art that what they're after is something which is so expressive that they can sell the cigarette package even where non-Western alphabets are common, like Thailand. I'm told the Coca-Cola bottle is another example that—

POURNELLE: If you're looking for universal languages, the most obvious one is the universal traffic signs, which are everywhere. And perhaps even a more universal one, the figures on the T-shirts, with the four feet, two pointing up and two pointing down, which is perhaps the most universal symbol across the world. I'm not convinced I know what good it does to have conveyed that meaning. I even saw at a science fiction convention not long ago a T-shirt in which the two female feet pointing up were normal human feet and the two pointing down were obviously clawed beast feet and it said, "Close Encounters of the Fourth Kind." Once again, I'm not sure I understand whether that statement helps solve the problems that Mr. Berry puts forth.

HARDISON: Let me go back maybe one step to put some of this in perspective, at least as I see it. If you go to the National Gallery of Art, you see a painting saturated in history, which has a very tragic vision of man, symbolized most obviously in picture images repeated endlessly of the Crucifixion, Christ dying on the cross, but also, say, in the lined faces of the figures, the portraits painted by Rembrandt, etcetera. It's not all tragic; some of it is bathed in a very lovely quality, such as Botticelli's "Primavera," for example, or "Venus Ouranos." And that's a great experience. Then you walk across the Mall to an equally large building, the Museum of Air and Space. I think it was Myra Sklarew who said, "Isn't it marvelous, we're the only country in the world that has a museum of air and space?" And you go into that building, and you see very lovely Brancusi-like creations all around you. You also see strange spider-like creations like the lunar lander, which have a different but nonetheless very strong esthetic. But the one thing that is fascinating is that you seem to have stepped out of history. You can look at a German V-2 rocket and it's a beautiful shape, and you can admire the shape and somehow or other, as you are admiring it, you're not aware of what it was built for and the destruction that it caused. I suggest that we are moving on two levels, what I would call an esoteric and a mass level, into a culture increasingly dominated by a perspective closer to that of the Air and Space Museum than of the National Gallery of Art. Let me finish. A world in which nothing is permanent, obsolescence is very rapid, a world in which there is an increasing class separation between those who really understand what is going on and those who live in the world and experience and internalize in their consciousness what is going on. To those who really understand what is going on, say, a computer program is very obviously a computer program. To those who don't and see it, it's a dada poem like the poem that I included in my paper which I called a found poem entitled "Meditations of a Robot." It's a little list, program, for defining functions in artificial intelligence. For the great majority of people, a technological society is experienced as a world which is increasingly surrealistic, in which things are done to them and in which they are surrounded by shapes, all of which speak to them esthetically but which they don't really understand.

BERRY: Why don't you go the next step and say the explosion is beautiful.

HARDISON: Well, I think probably a mushroom cloud is beautiful, I don't see anything unbeautiful about it.

BERRY: But don't we have to make some distinctions?

HARDISON: Well, what distinctions would you like to make?

BERRY: Some moral distinctions, for one thing; a distinction about the differences in results of different things.

HARDISON: I think maybe you've touched on a very crucial issue; I agree with you.

BERRY: I think I have, too.

HARDISON: Are we moving in a direction in which traditional moral distinctions are really not as significant as they have been? Just a minute. Is this one of the reasons why certain people are claiming that language is worn out, that the old words get us to react in cliché manners and to revert to the Hemingway problem in World War I, that the people who react in these matters are basically being manipulated by forces that want to use these traditions for their own purposes?

BERRY: But why don't these new things you're talking about that are so dangerous simply revitalize the whole moral vocabulary?

HARDISON: I don't think they're entirely dangerous. You said "very impressive." We're not going to solve the problem of soil erosion without satellites, without infrared scanning, we're not going to solve it without genetic engineering, we're not going to solve it without very elaborate applications of engineering principles and geological principles and soil—

BERRY: No, not so. It's been solved in Peru for about four thousand years.

POURNELLE: I don't know that that's necessarily the case, and I'm probably the strongest advocate of high technology here. I am a little concerned about something. I want a man to act like he is an adult dealing with my daughter. I don't really care to have a man say that it makes him feel good to murder children, and thus, because it makes him feel good, it's a beautiful act and he's going to do it. This is what got me upset yesterday. I think that morality had better have some basis, more than just what makes you feel good right now, this afternoon. If intellectual activity is going to essentially say that if something is hackneyed and clichéd, you know, that we're forcing people to do things, and that's all there is to intellectual activity, then I guess I can just go back to writing thrillers.

WALD: I've heard Mr. Hardison's talk with the greatest of interest and pleasure. I wonder if I could comment on just a few passages. I'm a little bowled over by my companion, Mr. Berry, here, because when I leave this gathering a little early it is to fly to Cleveland to address a rally on trying to stop the arms race. So reality is very close, and when I listen to you I think of a favorite sentence: "One can gain knowledge from words but wisdom only from things." I'd like to make a few comments on things that came up in the course of Mr. Hardison's paper. One early on that's very important to recognize, and that there's enormous confusion about even among biologists: no living creature is the ancestor of any other living creature, nor, of course, has it been discarded. What we have to face is two views of the living world, that of Darwin and that of Goethe. And Goethe's view is perfectly correct; he was pursuing the idea of a number of what he called *foramen*. The amoeba has never been discarded, the amoeba is at the pinnacle of the evolution of amoebae. It is telling us how to be an amoeba; the worm, how to be a worm. And each of these forms that are contemporary with us is a pinnacle form. There has been no discarding; they are not among the bones, they are among the fruits of evolution. Another comment: I think what you said at one point, Mr. Hardison, was that science is telling us everything is provisional, sometimes expressed as everything's relative. It's not true that everything is relative; there are a few—I don't like to use the word *absolute* but—universals. So, for example, Pythagoras was right: there is nothing that is as beautiful an expression of the playing with numbers as the periodic system of the elements, and the periodic system of the elements is universal. How do we know that? We know that because wherever we can pick up light, from the most distant places in the universe, that light, resolved in the spectrum, reveals lines, absorption lines, emission lines, that tell us, yes, the same elements are there. It would just shatter our whole concept of what goes on if we found some new lines in this spectrum. In fact, two missing elements, missing on the earth, were found in the investigations of the spectra of starlight. So not everything is relative or provisional; there are a few anchors. It's very important, I think, to realize that. Primitive art. Abstraction is at its heart. Leaving abstraction behind is a rather late event in our own culture. There is that science of perspective of which western art became so proud, I think a violence committed upon art and its real functions. Let me say, as a scientist concerned with vision, if you want really to look at a perspective painting, always shut one eye. Perspective art is to be seen with one eye, because if you keep both eyes open, the one eye is telling the other that's a flat surface, and all the tricks of trying to give the illusion of three dimensions in two on a canvas are defeated by looking with two eyes. In the National Gallery in London there is, in fact, an object put together, I've forgotten his name, by a Dutchman, a contemporary of Rembrandt's, in which you look through a peephole and you seem to be looking into a whole succession of rooms, through doors, you see, completely furnished rooms and endless depth. You can go around to the other end of this thing and look through another peephole, and it's almost impossible to imagine that what you're looking at is, in fact, flat surfaces painted in perspective, but the peephole makes you look at them with one eye. Primitive art is all abstract, and it has another quality that my friend beside me, I think, is perhaps asking for, and that is meaning. And its meaning is largely its content of *mana;* it's what we think of as magic. It's an art meant to change the course of events. It's an art meant to do work in the world, and indeed I think that's the highest function of all art, yes, to stir emotions, to convey, to be evocative, to convey associations, all those things, but also, surely, to do work in the world. This world needs that work very badly when art relinquishes meaning, and I think the word *experiment* has many meanings. Experiment in science is an attempt to make nature speak intelligently. In an experiment one is asking a question, and if it's a well-designed experiment, one gets an answer, and then can ask the next question, with an experiment, to get the next answer. So one is in a conversation with nature. It's not escape from nature, it's not a departure from nature, it's a conversation with nature. A good experiment makes nature speak intelligently. So to me meaning is an essential in art. And the scientizing of art, I wonder—I'm about to stop but with a question: Does it ever produce a better art? I am thinking about perspective again, for example, which was an introduction, you understand, the visual artist, in a sense, like the scientist, is doing experiments with what? With relations of vision to nature. But if this becomes a kind of slavish reproduction—you know, I was astonished to see this coming back of superrealism into art. I think that is a violence to the art, in a way a subtraction of meaning from the art. I wonder whether scientizing art ever is to its benefit. I wonder whether we're not in another such complementarity situation, in which art and science are the two aspects of reality that need to be pursued, and art, to a degree, surely complementary.

BEALL: I think Dr. Hardison discussed part of this issue when he said that the culture makes individuals who then in turn make the culture. What I'm hearing from some of the people in the room is that the writers are apart from the general movements of the culture and the general movements of the society, and I guess, as a scientist, I don't feel that. I don't think, for instance, if I were to write a story about the abuse of children, like Genêt did, and paint in such a language, that it might be construed as art. I have the responsibility of the work, but the culture has the responsibility for it as well. No one of us acts alone, it seems to me, in our efforts to do physics. There is no ability that I have to perceive all of the consequences of my actions, and I have to have some implicit faith in the culture that I live in, as we all must, that there will be some discussion or some referendum or some decision about it that we'll make the best use of it that we can. We've made mistakes in the past, but we've made some good judgments as well, as a society. It's certainly an imperfect system, but my sense is that it's not as neglectful of the basic issues that we're all concerned with as it might seem at first.

APPLEMAN: I wanted to follow up some of the things that Wendell Berry was saying and some of the things that Dr. Wald has said, too. And I have a question that is addressed to everyone, and especially the scientists, and it's probably, again, too late to get an answer to this question, but maybe this afternoon, after we've thought about it awhile. It'll take me about two minutes to ask this question, because it involves making a few distinctions among kinds of experience. It begins with a couple of what may be controversial remarks, one being that it's now twenty-two years since C. P. Snow left us his essay called "The Two Cultures" (and I think it's inevitable that somebody mention it at a conference like this), in which he reminded us of what we knew at the time, that scientists and literary people were not talking to each other much and that when they did talk to each other, it was more literary people speaking to science in their off-hours—scientists were not much interested in literature when they were at work—and that literary people hardly ever listened to what scientists said, partly because they didn't understand them and couldn't. And he saw that as an unhappy situation, and indeed it was and, I gather, still is. The other possibly controversial statement would be that whenever we do talk about science and literature, we generally mean that in some way science is affecting literature and not the other way around. Something Wendell Berry was implying may not be altogether proper, but it probably is the case. Carl Sagan says that Goddard got interested in Mars and then he started making rockets, but I have a feeling that Goddard would have made rockets whether or not he was a science-fiction fan. And there simply are not very many instances that I know of in which a literary person has influenced a scientist in his work, however much he may have changed his life or made it more enjoyable. But there are three distinctions that I'd like to make, and out of these distinctions I would like to ask a question about the last item, because that's what I'm really interested in. I need to mention the other two in order to exhibit what I'm not interested in. One of the first kinds of influence science has on literature is simply to horrify the literary person with what's going on in science. We see that with some frequency in all kinds of literature, but Dr. Hardison mentioned Eliot, and Eliot has been mentioned a couple of times here. Eliot was horrified at science because what he saw coming first out of Darwin and then out of Sir James Frazer and also Jesse Weston was something that he didn't understand, and so far as he understood it, he was terrified. And it came at a point in his life when he was going through difficulties in his marriage and a nervous breakdown and the death of a very good friend, and it sort of led him to a poem, the only appropriate epigraph for which he thought was Conrad's "The horror, the horror." Interestingly enough, exactly the same thing happened to Tennyson a hundred years earlier, when Tennyson had just finished reading Miles's *Geology* and his best friend Arthur Hallam died and led him to a poem that became "In Memoriam." The rejection of science, the turning away from science, is simply the appalled response to science that literary people have had for a couple of centuries, ever since about the aftermath of Newton. Newton was the last scientific person to whom all of the poets turned with great approbation. "And God said, 'Let Newton be,' and all was light." That was the last favorable thing we've heard from the literary people toward science. And now we've had two hundred years of hostility. I've got two other things to say, and I promise to be quiet. A second kind of convenient literary response to science is what we get in science fiction, which is very frequently not a response to science in the relatively pure, abstract sense of experimental science but a response to hardware. What you read is technology fiction; you get basketfuls of technology and very little of what might be called science in the other sense of the word. And for that reason, it's sometimes fun and titillating but often not really very interesting. It's Chinese food, you know, you go away and you're hungry again an hour later. I am not all that much taken with a lot of science fiction for that very reason, and when you get a science fiction writer like Ursula Le Guin, who goes beyond that and uses science in ways that really are intriguing in terms of human nature, her superiority to the others is immediately recognized. Those two categories of things are not what I would like to have as answers to the following question. What I would like to ask you—particularly the scientists—is the question I ended up asking Dr. Wald yesterday. Where in our literature today, insofar as we have poets, novelists, and dramatists who are interested in the world they are living in, and in the way Wendell Berry says we should be, who are living in the aftermath of a cultural revolution which has been led by science for four hundred years and in very dramatic ways for two hundred years, where is the literary response that seems to scientists competent or responsible? Let me give two examples that spring to mind and then be quiet. One is in the fiction of Thomas Pynchon, which very thoroughly absorbs certain principles out of physics. In *Gravity's Rainbow*, which lots of people start but few people finish, the whole book is absorbed with those principles. And in a very famous short story called "Entropy," Pynchon has absorbed the notion of the second law so thoroughly that it's not only a bit of hardware in the background, it goes right into the psyches of the people in the story—a perfectly marvelous example, it seems to me, of somebody writing real science in real fiction. And the only other example that comes to mind (I hope Mr. Berry will agree with me) is Gary Snyder, who is, in fact, an anthropologist. He has studied anthropology seriously and, as one of our best poets, has worked that material into his poetry in a complete way, so that we have a poetry of anthropology which reminds us of some of the responsibilities that Mr. Berry was talking about; respect for the land, respect for cultures, and so on. Besides those three examples, it's pretty thin work for me, and I would very much appreciate contributions from all the rest of you as to where you see this happening. You needn't tell me you haven't seen it happening, if you haven't, because I already know that, but if you've seen it working in someone other than Pynchon or Snyder or—okay, that's all I have to say.

POURNELLE: Sir Fred Hoyle's *Black Cloud* is a fairly decent book written by a fairly respectable scientist.

BERRY: In my concern with agriculture, I've run into several scientists with whom I have had considerable common ground and no trouble speaking. I don't know whether the influence has gone from me to them, but it certainly has gone from them to me, and I worked hard enough to see that it went the other way. But certain things seem to be necessary. One is that both sides speak common English. Another is that both sides have to have some concern, some sense of consequence. Both sides have to have some particular care for some particular place and group of people or community. There has to be an avoidance of the grandiose in scale; a small enough scale so that it's translatable. I don't really see how you could translate from the concerns of a power company nuclear physicist to the concerns of any writer I know.

MEREDITH: We have a few minutes left. I think some of us could contribute to a bibliography of the kind that Philip Appleman speaks of. There's a book by Russell Hoban called *Riddley Walker* that was reviewed recently. It speaks directly to our concerns, because what is scientifically experimented with is the English language as it would survive two thousand years from now, after the culture that it derives from has been obliterated, or almost obliterated, by an atomic war. The book is set in the vicinity of Canterbury, and the two sources of power, with which language is trying to wrestle in the post-nuclear holocaust era, are the archbishop of Canterbury, who is a vestigial descendant, and a scientific leader, who is a vestigial descendant, and they are primitive people speaking a primitive language. This is to me the same kind of thing that Pynchon does: it deals with literature and science, and the science that's involved here, I suppose, is linguistics. But that is, indeed, a science, which is apart from literature. It's a much more profound attempt to deal with this than, say, Burgess's attempt in *Clockwork Orange*, to deal with it, the language as it has evolved. But do any people have books they want to tell us about?

RODDENBERRY: I wanted to suggest that there is an area of language that we haven't mentioned and with which many of the things we're talking about are very concerned. This is the new language of telecommunications, which may do as much to obliterate the culture as the atomic bomb, in some ways. But it's a combination of sound and image in which cinematography and camera movement and form and color and all of these combinations are really creating in front of us here and will, obviously, even more so in the future, create a new language. And I think that to define language as only a printed thing does not allow us to think of all of these concerns in relationship with today and tomorrow, where we're going and what's happening.

MacLEAN: Language is very crippling. It's subject, predicate, subject, predicate, subject, predicate; you just have to wait forever to get it. And this was probably what Joyce was trying to get around; he's got what is like a musical score, several things going on at the same time. Language is like a horse eating, it's endless. You always have to wait to get to the last word. And so you're absolutely right. The brain, particularly the neocortical part, likes to see several things going on at the same time instead of waiting forever to get to that last sentence. But, on the other hand, when you get to making love or eating or doing any of these other things, it's sort of nice to go at this slow pace, you see. So we have these combinations of animals inside us that we're all having to satisfy at the same time. I loved your presentation.

POURNELLE: I think there are several unstated assumptions here, and I'm not sure that I buy a couple of them. Furthermore, I'm not sure that you do, either, because there's obvious conflict between the definition of literature as it seems to be used most of the time here and what Dr. Wald said is literature, which is that it does work in the world, that it influences people to do things. As a datum, the devil writers don't influence science. You go out to JPL: about 30 percent of the people who are on staff out there made their career choice largely as a result of having read the novels of Robert A. Heinlein in their youth. Now, you may not call Mr. Heinlein's—

[UNIDENTIFIED]: What's JPL?

POURNELLE: Jet Propulsion Laboratory. I use it as an epitome of a high-tech center. It's a place that the images come from Saturn and so forth. Now, you may, as Mr. Appleman, I think, decried the influence of Mr. Heinlein. Some of you may say that's not literature. But what do you mean, it's not literature? Anything that influences the world as much as those books have has got to be something. It certainly has enormous influence. I have fairly high influence. My books are fairly widely read; they sell a lot. They are read, in large part, by the technical community. I write a column. I don't agree that literature has no influence over science. I find it a very peculiar thing that stuff that is produced by random processes can be called literature and art, whereas a deliberately crafted book that is intended to sell a couple of million copies and does, in fact, accomplish that goal, is not art. I think Gene Roddenberry's "Star Trek" has had more influence over the world than every one of us in this room put together. I think that you are dealing with one of the most influential people in the world down at the end of the table there. And on the other side of the picture, the controversy that Sir Fred is engaged in with regard to Big Bang versus continuous creation is probably one of the most important questions in the world. Now, we have people who are, it seems to me, involved in important concerns. Professor Wald, here, for all that I do not agree with his politics, is working on, in my judgment, one of the most important things in the world, which is, how do we stay alive. And Mr. Berry is. But, you know, in order to conserve soil, you have first to decide that you want to, which means that you have to decide that there is a future, and that that future is sufficiently attractive as to make you forego pleasures today in order to preserve that future. And it seems to me that's what literature is about. That's what art is about. To the extent that we are doing anything worth doing, we're trying to tell people that there bloody well is a future, that it can be a good one, and that you have to work to bring it about and not eat the seed corn.

WALD: Suppose that future is incompatible with the existence of the Jet Propulsion Laboratory?

POURNELLE: That is a question worth debating, and at least we have got to something that is discussable as opposed to this vague dadaist kind of—

HARDISON: Could I comment on that, since assumptions have been questioned here. I think, really, there is a difference of opinion around the table about what is literature. First off, let me say that when I talked about reading Darwin and D'Arcy Thompson as literature, I myself thought I was giving the broadest possible definition to literature. I certainly would not exclude "Star Trek"; I don't even exclude the Virginia Slims cigarette package from literature. Second, what is the function of art, be it literature or painting or music or anything else? I tried to summarize a point of view which seems to me to be a valid one. It is a way of helping us see and understand. At times, what it helps us see and understand is not very pleasant. At times, you have to confront the paradox that things that you might find morally repugnant are characterized by qualities that may seem beautiful. I once visited a hospital in New Jersey in which, in the anteroom, there was a series of huge enlargements of photographs of cancer cells—and they were decorations hung around the room. I had to read the fine text to learn that they were cancer cells, because they didn't look like cancer cells. They looked like abstractions, paintings, and some of them were quite remarkable, some of them, I would even say, were beautiful. But I don't even think beauty is the essential element of art; I think it is its ability to help us see and understand who we are and where we are. If art does that, it's performing its fundamental mission. I think an art which becomes propagandistic, which tries to serve socialist realism or tries consciously to serve soil erosion or tries consciously to serve the improvement of the moral standards of teenagers (let me say, parenthetically, that I have four daughters, and I certainly did not imply, or intend to imply, in my earlier comments, that I want to attack morality)—I think an art that consciously sets out to attack morality is as corrupt as art which consciously sets out, as propaganda, to defend or espouse a certain cause and is willing to surrender its claim to producing the truth as far as the artist can offer it in order to be propaganda. I find propaganda art characteristic of totalitarian societies. I find the urge to convert art into propaganda characteristic of some of the movements in the United States in the twentieth century that I feel are least attractive and may be most threatening. But I think that art is a way of helping us to see and understand, and when it does that, it's performing its function.

APPLEMAN: The reason I took several minutes to put the question I put to you was so that I could make several distinctions that would avoid the kind of answer that Mr. Pournelle gave. I am still interested in the question that I am talking about; I am not interested in hardware. I am interested in science and how science comes into literature in a different way. So my question to the company remains, perhaps for this afternoon.

MEREDITH: The session this afternoon, which begins at 2:30, after our lunch in the Whittall Pavilion, will be chaired by Dr. Jim Beall, and he will not tell you who he is, but he has had a great deal to do with making this conference possible because science and literature have acquired some rudimentary suggestions about science, and he's the only person that Maxine and I know who has really worked with us who has this equipment. He will moderate and [I will] have things that I couldn't say as moderator about O. B.'s paper, but I will be able to say them then, and we will, at this point, have no lectures but only the most sincere kind of argument. It is, I think, encouraging and exciting that there are real differences developing because that's what we're here for. We're not here to agree with one another, but to talk about omissions and failures of communication between the disciplines. The reason that most of the poets were struck dumb and the poets who spoke spoke not of poetry is that we have, still, I think, to make connections with a subject that was brought up this morning. And I hope this afternoon we can do that bettter. We thank Dr. Hardison.

SESSION 3
November 10, 1981

*The Outlook for Science and Literature:
Open Discussion*
JAMES BEALL, Moderator

BRODERICK: You heard all about Jim Beall this morning, so I won't bother to introduce him. He is our moderator for the afternoon.

BEALL: We have quite an agenda for ourselves in terms of territory to cover. I would like to do a couple of things. Some people pointed out that we hadn't really formally introduced ourselves, and so I thought, very quickly, we could go around the table and just say our names and where we're from so that people can attach names to faces, for those who haven't spoken an enormous amount. My name is Jim Beall.

MS. KUMIN: Maxine Kumin.

MEREDITH: William Meredith.

MR. KUMIN: Victor Kumin.

POURNELLE: Could people include about a one-sentence tag as to who or what they are while we're doing this? Because the names by themselves don't really help a lot.

BEALL: Here I make a point of order: literally one sentence. I am a physicist and I also write poetry.

MS. KUMIN: I am the consultant in poetry at the Library of Congress.

MEREDITH: I am a poet.

MR. KUMIN: I'm a chemical engineer; my name is Victor Kumin.

SKLAREW: I am Myra Sklarew; I studied science and I teach literature.

MICHAEL GLASER: Michael Glaser; I'm a teacher and a poet.

PASTAN: Linda Pastan, a poet.

APPLEMAN: Philip Appleman, poet.

MERRILL LEFFLER: Merrill Leffler, former engineer, teacher of English, and I write poetry.

POURNELLE: I'm Jerry Pournelle, I used to be head of Human Factors for NASA. I write novels and I buy poetry.

BERRY: I'm Wendell Berry, a writer and a farmer.

LEFCOWITZ: Al Lefcowitz, professor at the U.S. Naval Academy and director of the Writer's Center, D.C.

DIANE ACKERMAN: Diane Ackerman, poet.

PATRICIA GARFINKEL: Patricia Garfinkel, poet, and I work with science during the day as a speechwriter.

NANCY GALBRAITH: Nancy Galbraith; I'm in the Poetry Office here at the Library.

ALENIER: Karren Alenier; I'm a poet and a computer specialist.

SARGENT: I'm Bob Sargent, poet.

RICHARD SELTZER: Richard Seltzer, and I write novels and make a living by working for a computer company.

HARDISON: O. B. Hardison; I am the director of the Folger Library across the street.

RODDENBERRY: Gene Roddenberry. Believe it or not, I was once aiming to be a poet but got trapped by television.

POURNELLE: You're the most successful poet in the room.

STEPHEN BARATZ: Stephen Baratz; I'm a clinical psychologist working on Einstein's model of thinking as it relates to peace.

MacLEAN: Paul MacLean, I'm in brain evolution and behavior at the Laboratory of Mental Health, National Institute of Mental Health, and I use metaphors occasionally.

WALTER JAMES MILLER: Walter James Miller, poet and science writer.

HOYLE: Fred Hoyle, theoretical physicist and astronomer by adoption.

POURNELLE: Damn good novelist, too.

JOSEPH PRICE: I'm Joe Price, and I have the good fortune to be in charge of our collections in science and technology here in the Library of Congress.

LAD: Pramod Lad; I'm a biochemist.

RUTH BOORSTIN: Ruth Boorstin, writer.

CAROLINE MARSHALL: Caroline Marshall, writer, teacher.

ANN KELLY: Ann Kelly, teacher, and I'm working on Jonathan Swift, who was very interested in the relation of language and science.

BRODERICK: I'm John Broderick, and, as all of you know, I write letters and sign travel vouchers.

BEALL: My official position here today is moderator, and with some sense of responsibility for that I'm going to refrain from making too many pronouncements. I would, however, like to give the first two moderators, who so graciously directed our discussions and arguments, an opportunity to speak in their own behalf, since they no longer have to worry about their responsibilities to moderate. Maxine?

MS. KUMIN: No, I'm going to pass for right now, I'll take you up on that later.

MEREDITH: I wanted to speak to the discussion this morning, and Wendell Berry said the things that I would have tried to say the first time around, but the second time, when I wanted to say, about the extremely interesting paper, the best thing I've ever read about dada, concrete poetry, and algorithmic poetry, making the point that they are a single manifestation of a response to scientific discovery, what I wanted to say about that is that I share with O. B. the feeling that poems are supposed, as John Berryman says in one of the "Dream Songs," these poems are not to be understood, you understand, they are only meant to terrify and comfort. That's what poetry does, and what I feel about the examples given is that they don't terrify and comfort. They are, in fact, like most of the work of those three separate elements, intellectual solutions to a problem which requires a felt solution, and that, if I want to know what kind of trouble I'm in, I don't go to the avant garde poet, I go to the poet, like Berryman or Lowell, who takes me by the throat and says, "This is really what's happening," and often he takes me by the throat by using devices that have not changed much since the Elizabethans. This brings me to points which I will make seriatim, the orderly way Mr. Appleman makes them, although my mind is not that orderly. One is that our selves have not essentially been changed; the person that George Wald describes, the human animal striving to reckon with its own consciousness, is pretty much continuous from Homer to now. The second point, I guess, is that our language, save for modifications which the poets, by and large, come up with, is the language of the tribe. These are noises which have accumulated meaning through the experience of millenia, and, in the case of the *Oxford English Dictionary* we have a relatively brief account of our own tongue, but it is not anything that anybody wants to say has been supplanted by modern linguistics or by the modern science of poetry. And the third element which it seems to me is not new is the poetics of our art itself. The poetics don't go out of date; there is no new theorem which contradicts Dante. Everything that's been said in the arts that was ever true is still exactly as true, subject to no revision whatever. And because of this I think we must be careful about innovations which are not truly original, which, in fact, do not use the sensibility that comes from our consciousness and our past and which fail, somehow, to make a new point. The poetic revolutions—Wendell Berry spoke about Dante—all the recent poetic revolutions that we know about are attempts to restore language to what it was before. Wordsworth, Whitman, Frost, William Carlos Williams, Allen Ginsberg, in their different ways, have all been saying, not that we want a new poetry: we want the poetry of Blake or Li Po, we want the poetry of Shakespeare or Dante, we want poetry which relates to things as men speak of them. And this is my feeling about these experiments, that they were false analogies, by and large—very exciting, but the reason that I find that we don't have to take them as an exact parallel with the sciences is simply that they are not useful, they are not poems which help us to see our lives and our morality clearer through the introduced variations of our circumstance.

BEALL: It occurs to me that one of the things that's been asked is whether or not poets and artists and scientists have a responsibility to their culture for what they produce. I'm wondering if there is an interest in discussing that some more. It's obviously been addressed to a certain extent, and I think that it bears some further discussion. We are here to talk about science and literature, and I think this is a very important aspect of that. Wendell?

BERRY: Yes, I think there's been one issue that's come up two or three times that I've wanted to say something about or hoped somebody else would say something about, and that is the concept of "terrible beauty" or "terrible truth." There are beauties and there are truths that are just awful, and you can hardly stand it. Of course, one thing that art has done is to help us to stand those things. But the dangerous thing is that once you understand that there are certain things, certain beautiful or true things, that are at the same time terrible, that you will then set out to cause, or create, terrible beauty or terrible truth. Now, I think this is analogous to the discovery, which we all make sooner or later, that hardship is good for people. We know that it is, that people learn a lot from hardship and they probably even need it. And yet, once having discovered that hardship is good for people, we dare not then go out and instigate hardship for other people in order to help them out. So, again, I'm back at the issue of responsibility. I think that Yeats's "Easter 1916" poem is a monumental poem and almost an unbearable one and, at the same time, a very bearable one in that it's that paradox that we're interested in. But we credit Yeats for the poem, for the fineness of it because he acknowledged the existence of terrible truth. And we distinguish between him and Hitler because Hitler caused terrible truth. I think science is in a similar situation. Scientists have to distinguish, in my opinion, between acknowledging and understanding terrible truth and causing it; I think they have caused more than their share of it.

MEREDITH: There is a sentimental presumption, I think, in modern literary criticism, that unless your work is terrible, it can't be very serious.

POURNELLE: Worse than that, I have seen literary criticism which essentially says that unless something recognizes the fallen and irretrievable state of man, it cannot be literature. I have seen that published, and apparently with some accolade from the academic profession as being a truth about literature, and I think it's bullshit.

RODDENBERRY: Once you begin insisting that the artists of any type share responsibility for this or have a sense of where humanity is, I think it's so obvious that the very act of art is an intensely selfish and personal thing. And once you begin laying those other roads down, you diminish the quality of art that your society produces, as much of it is produced for intensely selfish reasons.

HOYLE: The question that's been raised, I think, by Dr. Appleman this morning, about the responsibility of scientists for their discoveries, and at the risk of raising the hackles of the meeting, I'm willing to say, yes, scientists do have a responsibility and they pretty well completely discharge it. I think a lot of the feeling against science is really a feeling against the universe, that the universe is the way it is. I've had this, just this same debate with a friend whose name may be known to many of you, J. B. Priestley, and Jack always takes the view that, why is it always this way? Why don't we stop it? Well, the point is you can't really stop it, because that's the way the world is. And if, for example, one were to take an extreme religious point of view and say that there is a God and God created the universe, then the facts on which science is based is the word of God. I mean that would be to take an extreme point of view, but this is the way it is. And I have a feeling that when we refer to two cultures, it's not really science and nonscience, or literate culture, that we have there, because, quite evidently, there are many people on the literary side who are entirely competent to deal with numbers and so on, so Snow was wrong in this. It's really a clash between an older culture and a more modern one, and the old culture really doesn't like what the modern culture is revealing. And I don't think we can turn the clock back and say we would like to go back five hundred years; there is no way, this is the way the universe is. If we turn our back on it, we're really stopping the very process that has taken us from swinging in trees, because that is what the human animal is, to find out about the world. Now, let's come to the question of responsibility for what is discovered. Well, everybody has in mind the nuclear bombs—this has been mentioned two or three times around the table—and I think the idea that is in people's minds is why is it, when these dreadful things are discovered, that people continue to work on them? There is a trap here, for all of us, in the nature of things, that once a discovery is made, it becomes ten times as easy to apply that discovery as it was to make the discovery; it becomes dead easy to apply the discovery. So it really is a question that once the discovery is made, it cannot properly be suppressed. I think one has to accept it. It's very much like the Garden of Eden; once the fruit of the Tree of Knowledge has been eaten, you can't put the clock back any more, because anybody can do it once the facts are known. What I think the true responsibility of the scientist is is to make the facts known to people at large, to everybody. And I think in this respect scientists have discharged their responsibility. They have fought tooth and nail against governments to stop crucial information being buried in secret reports. This has run all the way through since the end of the last war. Even the Russian scientists have finally managed to win that battle around the middle 1950s; they fought it very hard. So that in the sense that the information is provided for all of you, if you're on the literary side, it's there, I think that responsibility is being discharged. And I then think it's up to all of us, particularly in our kind of society, to elect the leaders who are going to apply this knowledge in the way they see fit. I mean, particularly writers, you should be extremely influential in deciding what kind of leaders are appointed and how they should apply their discoveries. So I would say that, insofar as we make it known what are the possibilities in genetic engineering, we are essentially discharging the responsibilities. And these fellows who kind of work in the background on these problems once the discoveries have been made, I think that's really a very peripheral sort of issue, and I would like to be able to stop it, but it's too easy, once the discoveries have been made, really, to be stopped.

ACKERMAN: What do you see is the corollary responsibility of the writer?

HOYLE: Oh, well, your responsibility is to assess the facts, just the same as the scientists', and to say what you feel about the way society should go. And, insofar as you're more skillful with words than the scientists, you should have a bigger influence.

BARATZ: Why is writing a different type of art than painting?

ACKERMAN: Could I just follow up by asking, then, why, at a time when it is very popular to be a writer—under every rock there is a poet—are so few writers interested in nature as it is revealed to them through science?

POURNELLE: But is that true?

ACKERMAN: I think it is.

LEFCOWITZ: Yes, it is true.

POURNELLE: Science fiction accounts for some 40 percent of the publishing budget of the United States. The only category of fiction that's bigger is bodice-rippers.

ACKERMAN: Well, I do have to say that I'm not referring to science fiction. I'm referring to speculative fiction and poetry.

POURNELLE: Well, that's what I meant, the general category as understood by publishing, and 40 percent of the revenue of the publishing industry in the United States is the category "science fiction." That includes fantasy, what Harley Ellison called speculative fiction, spec fic, sci-fi, whatever you want to call it, that's 40 percent of the publishing industry, that's no small thing.

MS. KUMIN: But we're not talking about commercial fiction, we're talking about—

POURNELLE: Oh, if it's successful and reaches a lot of readers, it can't be literature.

MS. KUMIN: That's your definition, not mine.

LEFCOWITZ: It may turn out to be literature. I'd like to take it at another angle, which seems to be a dilemma for both the artist and the scientist, who in a way are both artists or both scientists—the modern dilemma: consciousness, that is, knowing, which allows us to move toward some kind of action. And I think this fits into what O. B. was saying this morning. First is the problem of self-consciousness, which is awareness of ourselves as aware instruments, which leads us somehow into inactivity, in part on the basis of, I think, a false analogy, at least on the artist's part, between the scientific work and the literary work. And the question that you raise about the literary reaction to science, it seems to me, is every bit as true of the scientist. The influence of science scared the shit out of us, but it scared the shit out of the scientists too, because of self-consciousness about what it could mean—that part of science which has become linked to technology, which the person in literature has used either as subject matter or has used to, again, scare the shit out of himself, which the scientists have done. And then, your third question is, what is the competent literary response? I'm not sure, obviously, that I can answer it, but I am fairly sure that one of the literary responses over the last two centuries of the growth of consciousness has been in fact a turning back on self, an eating of one's own tail. A turning back into a literary form on the part of the scientist as artist has been a separation from society, the very processes of that separation leading to the scientist finding an area of abstract knowledge in which [he has] to say, "I'm not morally responsible." The people who control the institutions, who have been in one way or the other, according to my studies, trained in the literary tradition, have said, "You're off someplace else. You're researching knowledge of some other sort. You go ahead and do your thing." And it seems to me the scientists may have given up their responsibility as artists, maybe for the last ten years, by accepting that role and saying, "I don't have any responsibility." The artist is also not taking any responsibility for science, because it, too, has been walled off into some area of pure knowledge. And so what we get is this very curious agreement to separate, which gets us back into the two cultures, but the two cultures, I think, from a different angle.

BEALL: So what you're suggesting, then, is that scientists have walled themselves off into their specializations and don't talk outside of them, which is true. Pramod Lad and I are both scientists, and when we talk, we talk about poetry. We don't talk about our research work. So scientists have walled themselves off into their specializations just as artists and writers have walled themselves off into theirs.

BERRY: I would like to say something about why people perceive scientists the way they do. It's not because they are backward people and scientists are advanced people. It's because most people don't have very much power or money, and when scientists appear before them, it's usually in league with large concentrations of power and money. And I'll give you a story. They're building a nuclear power plant twenty miles from where I live that has been publicly disgraced over and over again in the press for bad concrete, for telling the workers to not talk to inspectors, and that sort of thing. Enough stuff has been proven on the corporation and its contractor to put a private citizen in jail several times over, with the consequence that they're going right ahead and building a nuclear power plant. Now, a few months ago there occurred a public hearing at Madison, Indiana, in which a number of scientists and engineers having to do with the nuclear power industry appeared before the people of Madison, Indiana. Now, you're talking about making facts and making information available to people; these people were talking sheer scientific gobbledegook. Nobody could understand it, and the effort obviously was to intimidate people who had not that specialized information into silence and acquiescence. At one point in the proceedings, an inspired lady stood up and asked them to please raise their hands if they were from anywhere near that community. There were thirty-five or forty of them on the stage, all probably making an annual salary higher than most people in the audience, all allied with a juggernaut that's all but invincible, and not a one of them raised their hand. So people perceive scientists as a privileged group of aliens who are colonizing mineral-rich and energy-rich areas of this planet. And they have, in my opinion, a lot of explaining to do.

LEFCOWITZ: Let me comment on that. Isn't that the exact same thing you're saying about writers? In terms of Vonnegut being in some library, I mean, these kinds of power struggles go back, I suppose, to Pharaoh.

MS. KUMIN: But Vonnegut is not putting up a nuclear power plant—

LEFCOWITZ: But from their point of view, he is doing something that is as immediate to them in terms of their moral and daily structure. He is teaching them dirty words, and on one level at least, this is as meaningful to them as any other level. What we're dealing with, I think, is two cultures that have separated themselves from a third culture, and that has become a problem.

MS. KUMIN: The third culture, Al, involves all of us, that's the trouble, you see. I mean, we're all going to go together, the apocalypse is at hand, and it seems to me that all of us who are writers at this table have a moral obligation to begin now to be more *engagé* with the world we live in. I don't think we can afford the kind of narcissistic, sterile fragmentation of language that we see in concrete poetry, in dadaism, in what I see as the decadent outburst of a world that's ending. You know, we're all about to arrive at the hole, and this has happened over and over. Every time. Just before World War I, we get dadaism; just before World War II, we get a new outcropping of surrealism; and just before the final conflagration, it seems to me, we get this splintering off, in which the writers are all crawling back into one little cave and the scientists are over somewhere else, and there's no dialogue between the two, to speak of.

POURNELLE: Could I get the floor so Sir Fred can have it? He's not aggressive enough, and I am. I want to hear him.

HOYLE: I would like to answer Mr. Berry by saying that our point of view is just the opposite; we think we have no influence at all. I think it is really true that in no government anywhere in the world is a position of appreciable importance occupied by a scientist, and can you think of any other profession for which this is true? Think of the number of lawyers in the world's governments.

BERRY: The President's science advisor is not an insignificant position in this country.

HOYLE: It's a pretty minimal position.

PRICE: But I think his point is well taken, though, because, you see, the situation you describe, Mr. Berry, could very easily have been scientifically conversant Madison-Avenue-trained front men. I mean, I really don't know, but I know that some of this goes on, too, and the question is a definitional one. Are there any scientists—

BERRY: Let me phrase that the opposite way. I've been in a good many environmental fights, and I have never been in but one where there was a professional-grade scientist on my side. So if they're not for the government and not for these big collections of power, where are they and what are they doing?

HOYLE: As to the nuclear power plant, I would be on the opposite side from you, because I don't believe the next generation or the generation afterward should die of hypothermia. And so I would be in principle opposed to you.

Now, where I might have a point on your side is that this country has elected to build its nuclear power plants in a kind of dialogue between the government and private industry, and that may conceivably cause the sort of troubles that you mention, and I don't know the facts. Maybe the concrete is bad, I don't know. And I think an administrative mistake was made here to divide the responsibility for power plants between the government and private industry, and it would have been much better to have left it entirely under the government, as other countries have done. But that I regard as not a very fundamental point, although, of course, it may lead to a lot of individual troubles. I don't really think it affects the relation of science to society in a very deep sense.

BERRY: All right, take the shale oil industry; this was a technology developed by scientists, right? Nobody else could develop it. As soon as it's developed—now, I live in a state that's been strip-mined, and I know what I'm talking about—as soon as the possibility of so-called synfuels comes about, first we've got a big concentration of interest in the government, in the state government, in that, and the next thing that happens is representatives of oil companies are going around the state buying oil shale leases from farmers at what amounts to theft without any restrictions at all in the deed and for nominal sums. Where were the scientists and what was their responsibility? It seems to me that they should have been telling the people.

BEALL: I don't think you can ask individual scientists to be responsible for all of the activities of the culture.

BERRY: No.

POURNELLE: But some, certainly. There's no question about it that the scientists have some obligation to clean up their own bloody act.

GAIL MARCUS: There are always scientists on every side. You can get eight Nobel Prize winners for nuclear power and eight Nobel Prize winners against nuclear power.

POURNELLE: But oddly enough, the eight who are against it will not be physicists.

BERRY: Well, I'm telling you that in the fights that I've been in, and for a long time in strip mining, there weren't any scientists against it or with anything much to say about it at all.

HOYLE: But our problem is that the environmentalist treats the situation as if the world's population were about a fifth of what it is at the present. The tragedy is that the population has risen so high that, to avoid collapse, we have to do a lot of things—

BERRY: If we're to avoid collapse at present rates of consumption, we have to risk collapse from other causes. It doesn't make any sense.

POURNELLE: Do you want to run for office on that "less is better" platform? I notice that Jerry Brown gave it up, even, in California.

BERRY: It's not a question of whether anybody wants to run for office, it's a question of what's right.

RODDENBERRY: I think some stereotyping is going on here. I don't know where your community is, but in mine, scientists and writers are not in opposite camps; scientists have marched with us and marched against us and writers have done the same thing. I object to this stereotyping. It makes me want to put on a hula skirt and have a big cigar, because that's how producers look.

POURNELLE: We Californians just get along better.

MacLEAN: If any word or issue would characterize this conference, it seems to me that the word *responsibility* would, and it seems to me that responsibility as we know it goes back 180 million years ago, to the evolution of the family. Before that, we presume that the reptiles were eating their young, and the big quantum jump was the coming of mammals with the nursing, the modified sweat glands, the nipples and caring for the young, and, madame, we were talking about play; this is the big new thing with mammals, too. If the little ones are going to be flying around the nest, they can't be chewing each other up, so you have play. And then, through these elaborations of the greater formations of the brain, one sees responsibility generalizing to conscience, and this is what, it seems to me, you're all worried about. That's the music that comes to my ear. But poets, writers, and so forth, do they have any responsibility? Of course they don't have any responsibility, because their only responsibility is crying out. And this is another thing that one sort of has to remember: the little reptiles did not have an isolation call, because if they called attention to themselves, their mother would come and eat them up. But the way the little ones stay together on the deep floor of the forest, besides olfaction and vision, is the development of vocalization and hearing, greatly improved audio-vocal communication. And the isolation call is probably the most primitive of all vocalizations. I don't see why you sit around worrying about your responsibilities, because John Gardner, apparently, is hurting so much he couldn't even come here today. This crying out from inside to communicate with other people, other persons, other animals, other organisms. I've gotten to the age where I can't even pinch off leaves anymore, so this is why I look forward to getting out of brain research, so I don't have to go on maiming animals. But this is the big cry, as I see it, wanting to communicate.

BERRY: Aren't you responsible for telling the truth?

MacLEAN: Truth generalizes; I mean—

BERRY: There's no such thing as a lie, then.

MacLEAN: If you believe in the family, you don't need any other ethic to live by.

LEFCOWITZ: That is the paradox. The mushroom cloud can be beautiful, which can be a truth. We're asked to look at truth, and, on the other hand, as artists and scientists, we're asked to be *engagé*, and at times one obligation smacks into another.

BEALL: Pramod, did you have a comment?

LAD: Yes, I wanted to answer some of Wendell Berry's criticism of the scientist and why the scientist is perceived as being in league with the forces of evil and with big money and big power. There are a lot of things which are incorrect about this perception, and one of the basic things that's wrong with it is the way in which discoveries are made that lead to these dangerous applications. A scientist has the dilemma that he's working on a particular problem and it has a particular solution. When he finds that solution, he has the choice of sitting back and saying, "These are the possible ramifications, ten of which are good, three of which are wrong, and I will therefore, because some of them are wrong, I will abstain from publishing this, I will abstain from making this available to the world, and I will just sit back and do nothing." So the solution to him, then, is that the problem that he is working on will never be solved. Though it may be temporarily solved to him, it will make no contribution at all in the broader progress of what he is interested in. What happens is that once that discovery is published, and this is what Fred Hoyle is saying, a number of forces move in which then apply this particular discovery. I'll give you a particular example of this, the hybridoma experiment, published by Kohler and Milstein in England. They take a cell that makes one molecule and fuse it with another cell that divides, and therefore, you can immortalize a cell which divides and is committed to making a valuable molecule. Now, this particular experiment wasn't even patented. It's very doubtful either that Kohler or Milstein made a quick buck on it. Now, there are entire companies that have developed this particular concept. It's a cell fusion company, it's a fusion company, and so on, and they are multiplying, they are proliferating more than the cells were. And what has happened is that a simple discovery has now been taken over and by a number of forces to which Kohler and Milstein cannot possibly be held responsible. The same sequence of steps takes place in genetic engineering. If you look at the sequence of experiments, there are a number of technical problems, of how you can manipulate genes, and various solutions come together in what is now called genetic engineering. The people who made these discoveries could not at the time of making them or publishing them foresee all of the developments and be made deliberately to suppress them. The question is, what, then, should be done? One thing that can be done is that if there is a misuse of this particular technique, when discovery has become technique, and when technique has been adapted by industry and by forces of profit, then the people who have made it can go public and say, as Fred Hoyle said, that this is the misuse that is being made of our discovery. "Our discovery was made with this intent, and this is the use to which it is being put." The question is, what are the forces of the individual scientist emerging from his lab and not even having the necessary expertise to voice this criticism versus the forces which would combine to use it? And the answer is that the scientist always loses. For every scientist you will find on the podium who makes that big salary, you will find ten who are engaged in making those basic discoveries who are very underpaid. So this perception is a fundamentally incorrect perception about how discoveries are made or the intent behind them. You will, in fact, find many scientists involved, I know, in biological sciences who would be very sympathetic to your viewpoint, who would be very sympathetic with the protection of the environment, who care very much because they are affected by it as much as anyone. And insofar as they have the intellectual abilities to reason through very intricate problems, they would certainly be willing to apply those abilities on problems of more immediate concern to them.

BERRY: What's underpaid, would you give some figures?

LAD: What is underpaid? For which scientist? Anything, from $10,000 to $40,000, you will get a spectrum of salaries. You can ask, you can take any scientist at the National Institutes of Health and see what they are paid. It's the same structure as at the Library of Congress, okay? It's no different, if that's what you're getting at. Now, if you look at the salaries of industry, you could multiply that by 15 or 25 percent more. The mistake is that you're operating on the assumption that the very process of scientific discovery is wedded to some commercial process in which the scientist is committed to selling and to devising some horrible use for his discovery, and that is not true.

BERRY: Well, you're making a reasonable response to what I said. Nevertheless, the difference in point of view between us is very great. I'm speaking from a hinterland and you're speaking from a center, and, as I think you have to perceive it if you're from the hinterland, most causes are far removed from their effects. Most intellectual causes are far removed; now, I think the day is coming when scientists, like everybody else, are going to have to live with their effects. But, so far, there are mental air pockets between the understanding of the cause and the understanding of the effect.

HOYLE: But the trouble is that when the discovery is made, you don't know what the effect is going to be. It might be Alexander Fleming's discovery of penicillin, you see; that's the trouble. If you decide on a blanket rule to suppress everything, then maybe nine good things are lost for one bad thing.

POURNELLE: Let me give you an example of that, because it's one that you have to agree with or at least that you sat here and agreed with when it was said, which was, Professor Wald said that there was nothing more beautiful than this simplistic $E = mc^2$, but as a matter of fact, once you actually understand the implications of that, it becomes dead easy to make an atom bomb. The atom bomb is very much inherent in the 1905 paper, as I'm sure Sir Fred would agree, and it really didn't take a hell of a lot of ingenuity to deduce the one from the other. And yet we sat here and everybody in this room, as far as I can see, agreed, including Wald—I don't think there is anyone in this world who dislikes atomic weapons more than he does—and he is the one who said that it is one of the most beautiful things he had ever seen—the equation of $E = mc^2$—I heard him say it without challenge. But the fact is that the atom bomb is utterly deducible from that equation, and as Sir Fred said, it becomes dead easy to do it. It only now takes money.

APPLEMAN [?]: But where does that take you? I'm not sure.

POURNELLE: I'm not sure either, but I'm bloody sure it doesn't take you to suppressing things, because, as he said, what are you going to do, suppress Fleming too? Shoot unlicensed physicists? I have a series of stories on that subject—I make a lot of money on it—in which unlicensed physicists are taken out and shot.

BERRY: I'm not trying to say that they should be shot, but what I am saying is that I think scientists have to get into it with both feet; that is, they are going to have to, instead of going along with this notion of absolute progress, that everything that is discovered is a net gain, they're going to have to get into it and see that it's possible to misuse all these things, and real education about innovations has to have something to do with the moral issues of use.

MARCUS: When would we decide when to use anything? I mean, we still don't know what the effects, or how bad the effects are of carbon dioxide in the atmosphere.

BERRY: Well, one protection is to do things on a proper scale.

PRICE: I see part of your concern really as the nature and the success of public activism, because regardless of the issue, whether it's a scientific one or whether it's a social one or whatever, as you well know, in this country, things get done or don't get done based on the strength of personalities and what kind of forum or what kind of medium they choose to exploit. It's the science—pardon my word—it's the technique of public activism, and that's really, I think, what you're struggling with. I mean, you've personally, I'm sure, witnessed many instances where, perhaps, the needs and the sensitivities and the concerns of less powerful and less articulate people have just completely been run over and bulldozed by very strong, very powerful, and very well financed groups. But to criticize the effectiveness and the techniques of those groups is not, should not be confused with scientific or public policy issues or whatever. Anybody who has got the power and the money to get behind something can steamroll it, regardless of what it is. I think that's really what we're focusing on.

BERRY: I'm speaking out of an old concept, which is simply that humans can take too much power. They can take too much from each other, they can take too much from nature, and the definition of too much is the amount that they can't be responsible for.

HOYLE: This is the problem, ever since Plato, isn't it, it's how one runs a society, that's really what you're saying.

MEREDITH: I think in our moment the feeling of tribal unity is so minimal that I would suppose that there are scientists like George Wald and the Union of Concerned Scientists who probably represent a larger proportion of the scientific community than the socially responsible writers represent in our community.

POURNELLE: What does it mean to be "socially responsible?" I mean, you use this language of moral superiority, but what does it mean?

MEREDITH: People who do things like Wendell does, people who are politically involved in their communities—

POURNELLE: All right, but am I socially responsible? I also am politically involved in my community, and Wendell and I are on absolute opposite sides. The only thing we agree on is that there really is a moral basis to behavior and that ideas really have consequences, and that we agree on.

MEREDITH: There would be less harm done, and I say this with great generosity, there would be less harm done if there were more people like you than there are. Even though you are full of error, you are full of commitment. This is what I'm talking about—

POURNELLE: But I'm waiting to hear the errors exposed, by logic as opposed to just simply by definition. See, I am erroneous by definition—

MEREDITH: We are debating—

MS. KUMIN: You are noisy—

MEREDITH: One of us is wrong, but this is the way a democracy operates. As long as we can communicate with certain respect across the table, which I am not sure I feel much more of—

POURNELLE: I shall no longer be noisy anyway.

MacLEAN: Come back, Jerry, we almost lost you at dinner last night; sit down.

MILLER: I think the question of responsibility and control, and $10,000 to $40,000 and so on, words like this bring up a big question in my profession right now. If science is people who operate between ten and forty thousand, I want you to know that the Authors' Guild recently discovered that the typical American writer is earning so much that he qualifies for food stamps, even under the present qualifications. In 1885, George Moore said, "At the head of English literature sits a businessman." The question to me is, do writers have as much control of literature as scientists have of science? On our side, the literary side, we think they do, but probably they're both under the control of a system of greed, and that that is really what we're talking about. Every author who has published long enough knows, has gone through the experience that this particular book got a lot of advertising behind it because it got an early start in the sales, and the publisher took money from all the other books that he was putting out that month and put it on that book, and then five years later he went through the opposite experience. He had an equally good book, an equally necessary book, but somebody else's book got a two-inch head start, and his advertising money went over to that book. And when judgments in literature are made on that kind of process of greed, we wonder are they made that way in science, too? And if they are, then there's no real opposition between science and literature; science and literature should be joined against a common enemy.

MR. KUMIN: As an engineer, I'd view all this comment as being directed against me and feel quite guilty.

MILLER: My first book was called *Engineers as Writers*.

MR. KUMIN: I should read it, I suppose.

MILLER: I'll send you a copy.

MR. KUMIN: In defense, I guess, of the world of science, you should all recall, of course, the initial comment made about Einstein's theories of relativity and what they led to in the way of the development of atomic weapons and we should also recall that the process of developing an atomic weapon by the scientists was an extremely agonizing one. It was so agonizing that the legend is that they had twenty psychiatrists at Los Alamos to deal with the effects of a successful test of the atomic weapon. And that Robert Oppenheimer himself said that after the successful operation of these weapons and the end of the war, he congratulated those who participated in the process of developing the weapon and ending the war by saying, "I want you to look upon what you have done with both pride and compassion," and you've all read what Oppenheimer said, quoting Eastern mystics, his comment about "I have seen evil." Before the first test, he said to us, "There are many of us here who hope and pray that this test will prove to be impossible, that this concept will prove impossible to demonstrate; but if the test fails, we shall come back and work twice as hard in the remaining months available to us to make it work the second time." There's a kind of human schizophrenia involved in the process of science. In my own career, there was a great ennobling feeling about creating smokestacks in the name of reducing the penury of people in manual labor. We could increase the standard of living by improving the quality of manufacturing and by improving the quality and the quantity of manufacturing to make goods available at a lower cost to everybody and therefore lighten the burden to individuals who were tilling the soils by walking behind the plow which was drawn by a mule or a horse, one of Wendell's mules or one of his horses, perhaps. But in later reflection, of course, one sees that there are consequences of this that weren't anticipated, as Sir Fred pointed out. You can't always anticipate the consequences of your work. Einstein, I'm sure, didn't anticipate the consequences of his mathematical theories. And so, to blame the scientists or to assign the level of responsibility to the scientist is really, at the early stages of discovery, very unfair. And to blame the engineers for applying the work of the scientists, the discoveries of the scientists, is also very unfair, because if you peel an engineer, you will find a person. I'm more concerned today about the interface between literature and science, which is the subject of this symposium, and we seem to have gotten away from it; and I'm a little confused, I guess, by this morning's presentation as to why or where the root for communication between literature, at least as it was defined this morning, and science is. I don't think there is a bridge between that kind of literature and my kind of science. That's perhaps art, but it's not literature. As I pointed out to Dr. Hardison, I think I can get inspiration from that kind of art, but I get no guidance whatsoever. And literature, by my definition, is a kind of guidance system for the scientist, and in return is an equilibrium between the scientists and the writers, and science becomes a kind of guidance system, in a way, for literature.

ACKERMAN: It was suggested that the only literary responses to turn-of-the-century developments were reductionist, and that's not true, either. There were a lot of people trying to cope with that by accretion, not by trying to take a contingency sample of the big blooming confusion and reduce it to zero, but to try to accommodate as much of it as possible. People like Virginia Woolf, for example, or Dylan Thomas. There have been all kinds of responses to it. And I think the one sentiment that all the poets here have in common is bafflement at that kind of language, which isn't any more meaningful to us than it is to the rest of you.

MEREDITH: Yes, we talked about science fiction. People like Loren Eiseley and Dr. Lewis Thomas seem to me the most useful interface that exists, truly literate people whose writings engage everybody and who explicate the essentials of modern science without mystification. That kind of writing is terribly important. There is just enough of it that we know that it's what we need more of to talk across. And I think that we also need socially committed writers—anybody who has read Wendell Berry's book called *The Unsettling of America* knows that this kind of explanation of agriculture and sociology can come from a poet better than it can come from an agronomist or a sociologist. So we do have models of this, and it seems to me almost an act of civic responsibility that we should talk to one another across this particular arc of immediacy which comes from poets writing about science as they understand it, and scientists writing literately, as for the tribe instead of for themselves. Actually, the reassembly of America is going to come from some notion of tribal joining together again among various segments of our society, the least dangerous schism of which may be the one we represent here in this room. We are at least all educated to a point where we're ashamed of ignorance, and we're ashamed of disagreements which are arbitrary, so that we do want to communicate; therefore, it's half-done. But there are divisions in this country that can be healed, I think, by the understanding of progress in science and accomplishment in the arts.

LEFCOWITZ: Those schisms, it seems to me, are buried in our very institutions, our educational institutions and their rewards, by the very nature of our schools. And it seems to me that there's a failure of literature, since we've been talking about the failure of science, and that has been its failure to engage and effectively communicate the processes of science, because, to a large degree, as I see it, we're still wedded to an old cosmic view. Now, if literature is by its very nature conservative, perhaps we are on the trailing edge of wedding the old cosmic view to the new cosmic view and possibly wedded to an old morality. By and large, literature hasn't caught up. We're still blaming the scientists because of the scientists' failure to know the future and not accepting our own failure to understand the present. Our job as writers and scientists is to do the best we can in the present, accept the errors in the new cosmic view, and go with it. What we want is the predictability of that old dispensation, and we're not going to get it again.

RODDENBERRY: We're mixing a couple of things up, though; for example, take the social-political-economic system. That's one thing. Many of the swipes at scientists have really been commenting on that system. That's a thing apart from assigning necessary responsibilities to either scientists or writers. There's a smell of Jerry Falwell in that for me. I don't want anyone assigning my responsibilities. I think it's very dangerous for people to say, "Why don't you be responsible." I don't want Falwell's definition of responsibility. I don't want the Falwells to tell me what truth is and untruth. I think it's damned dangerous when we start pointing the finger at each other.

BERRY: Well, Falwell isn't the only one who has ever tried to tell you something.

RODDENBERRY: I'm just using him as an example, as a particularly upsetting example.

PRICE: Victor Kumin's remarks about literature perhaps providing guidance to scientists and scientists providing guidance to the writers of literary work posed a question in my mind which I just want to throw out. That implies value transference; in effect, guidance meaning an idea, values. And what I was wondering about, particularly in the modern world of specialization, with all that is being written by both groups, whether or not scientists actually are reading literature or whether all of our perceptions of the gap (or the bridge, whichever way you look at it) between these two groups, is not really shaped by our reading in magazines, in newspapers, in whatever, what someone else's perception is about this scientist or this writer. How much is that really shaping our perceptions of all these topics, and I don't have any answer to that question, I was just throwing it out.

ACKERMAN: I don't think that science is an endangered species right now. If you go to the newsstand, you see the most extraordinary number of popular-science magazines. The public in this country is involved in popular science with a religious piety that I think is extraordinary. But I do think that poetry is an endangered species. There is very little of it being read, and I wonder why this is happening. Why are people turning to science for the kinds of truths that they sometimes, historically, found in literature?

PASTAN: I want to talk just a minute about the responsibility of the writer and what his or her job is and address first Wendell, who says that the scientist must become more engaged, and Maxine, who says that the writer must become more engaged. I think that, as citizens, the writer and the scientist and the artist and the cook and everyone else has to become more engaged. The responsibility of the scientist is to do the best science he can, hoping to make discoveries that can make life go on longer and then throw it out, as Mr. Hoyle said, to everyone to do the best they can with. The writer has a more particular responsibility, and it isn't necessarily in political engagement. I think that what the writer can do by writing anything he's best at writing is to make the reader learn how to become more imaginative, to see and to feel and to make that imaginative leap between me and you, so that when he then comes as a citizen to make all the decisions that all of us are making in terms of what we do with nuclear power, what we do with other things, he can at least imaginatively have grown and learned how to feel, so that he'll, hopefully, come to the decisions that will lead to life rather than to death. But the scientist isn't more responsible for the particular political decision, nor is the writer. In a democracy, all of the citizens are supposed to become responsible. The scientists can open many paths, and the writer can sensitize people, so that, hopefully, they'll take the right path.

HARDISON: I'd like to speak to Linda's comment, and maybe reply to Victor in terms of the responsibilities of the writer, pointing out first that the artists that I talked about this morning represent only a minute, and rather transient, faction of twentieth-century literature, and I think you can find, if you want to go through literature in English, writers who express almost any values or point of view that you're interested in. These writers seem to me to be particularly significant for reasons I tried to express; but in terms of the responsibility of the writer and what the writer has to say, I'd like to read you a little passage from an English professor out in California named Ian Watt. He's a Britisher teaching out there, and he was talking about his experiences in Paris just after World War II. He says:

> In the talk I heard then, four new words struck me. I soon got tired of the first three—*engagé, authentique, absurde*—but the fourth, *la chose,* seemed somewhat less fly-blown. I started reading Francis Ponge's prose poems about things with enormous interest. I remember particularly a newspaper article about a talk Ponge had given called "Tentative Oracle." His attempt at a speech circled amiably about his dislike of the common hyperboles about literature, his sense of being sickened at the general theoretical and public propositions, and how, in his own writing, finding it impossible to put the great literary subjects into words, he had determined, like a man at the edge of a precipice, to fix his gaze on the immediate object, a tree, the balustrade, the next step, and to try to put that into words instead. It was a charming anti-talk, especially in its ending. "So we haven't had a lecture," he commented, "perhaps not. Why did you ask me?" Then he concluded, "Dear table, good-bye." At this, Ponge leaned over and embraced the table and then he explained, "You see, if I love it, it's because there's absolutely nothing in it which allows one to believe that it takes itself for a piano."

Now, let me read just the follow-up on that, because it's a serious point he's making. He's talking about his involvement in literature as a teacher, now. "I would like my own activities as a student and teacher of English to be as simple and yet comprehensive as that act. It should contain the same four necessary constituents: an intellectual recognition of just what I am modestly but directly attending to; an esthetic appreciation of the object of my attention for what it, exactly, is; direct communication, a commitment of my feelings to that object; and lastly, perhaps incidentally, an attempt to express all of the first three things in words." I think that the writer's commitment to give himself modestly but attentively to the thing before him and, when he commits it to words, to communicate it to other people, is his deepest responsibility, and not everything that everybody writes is going to appeal to everybody, but occasionally, as you leaf through various kinds of literature, you should encounter things that would speak to your needs.

BRODERICK: Let me add just a footnote to that. Isaac Singer read and spoke here at the Library last week, and, of course, his art is one of great simplicity and transparency and, yet, very wide accessibility. One of the things he shared with Ponge was that when he left his hotel room to go back to New York, he moved about the room and said, "Good-bye, room." So he had adopted that approach, just as you described.

HARDISON: I wonder, really, if there's anything in that summary, the second part of the quotation I read, which would be directly contrary to the attitude that a scientist would take to the little part of nature that the scientist is investigating.

HOYLE: I suppose we do tend to focus in on one particular thing and exclude the others whilst engaged on that particular problem. I can't speak too well, because my own system of doing research is to follow several problems, as it were, because this has the advantage, if one goes sour, one can jump onto another one. But I think, in general, what you say is right in the way that science is prosecuted by people sort of focusing in on the one thing.

BERRY: Do you mean ecologists will focus on one thing?

HOYLE: No. Except in ecology, at least. In that sense, one—

BERRY: Because ecology is everything.

BEALL: My sense of this is that we are talking about the social burdens of science and writing and that's appropriate; but when I do physics, I don't think of myself as being burdened by these great responsibilities. I like to do physics, and I have fun doing physics, and there's that element of playfulness which Paul mentioned earlier in this discussion. It seems as though writers and scientists are caught in the same basic box: we can't take ultimate responsibility for our activities. We are involved in the culture, and the culture will make use of what we do if we're not completely autistic, if we have any connection with the society at large. And I don't think you can ask an individual scientist or artist to take responsibility for everything that he or she does. But it occurs to me that there is also common ground in terms of the processes of our activities, and I'd like to know if there are any inclinations to discuss that, the actual need to play, to be involved in creative enterprises.

MILLER: One thing that Fred just said is important. I think good writers, like good artists and good musicians, also have several projects going at once, so that they can jump from one to the other, and I suspect you can always trace a lot of self-influence through all of those works. That's one process that certainly all creative people have stumbled upon.

MARCUS: One thing that's always struck me is the need in both fields for a lot of drudgery to follow on the creative inspiration. One percent inspiration and 99 percent perspiration is really common to both science and literature. The rewriting and rewriting again in the writing field, and the continual experimentation and refining of the experiment and the repeating of the experiment in the scientific field. It has often struck me that the two fields were not far apart in requiring the kind of person who can do those things and repeat them and see the value of that and follow through to the desired goal.

MILLER: Could I ask a question of the scientists? Does the writing up of their work ever lead them to new ideas about the work? In other words, is the writing classed as part of scientific thinking, too?

MARCUS: In a sense, I think that can be true. I find it more in preparing a talk than in preparing something written, because when I'm preparing a talk I'm preparing for any possible question anybody might ask me, even if it seems totally unrelated to the talk, and sometimes, in doing that kind of thing, I'll get off into an area I hadn't thought about before and explore something just in case I'm asked something in that area.

HOYLE: I would have said it almost certainly does. If one wants to do research in a new subject, the best policy would be to begin by writing a paper on it, and then one really learns it.

One really goes on duty as soon as one writes the paper, the process is far more intense, a great deal is learnt. But I think perhaps I might mention something connected with a famous Indian-American astronomer, Chandrasekar. He was asked to give an important lecture at the University of Chicago, which was normally given in the humanities. I think the intention was that he would speak about astronomy, but, being Chanda, he would naturally try to speak on the subject for which the lecture was intended, and he said to me, "The trouble is, I didn't know anything about the humanities, but I tried to learn, and the subject I decided on was to compare the creative careers of three people: Beethoven from music, Shakespeare from literature, and Newton from science." And he said that so far as the early periods and the middle periods were concerned, he could find almost no distinction at all in the creative process among the three. In the early periods, the chaps were really concentrating on breaking through in the world, giving the world what it wanted; in the middle process, the middle period, they were giving the world still what it wanted but doing it far better than anybody had conceived was possible before. But then, he said, as soon as one comes to the third period, it's instantly different. In the third period, the highly creative person becomes fed up with doing what the world wants, and so they begin to create out of their own imagination. And in Beethoven's case, he can write the late quartets, entirely something new, not conceived before. In Shakespeare's case, he can write *Cymbeline* and *The Tempest*. But what can Newton do? He can do nothing, because he cannot create a world out of his own imagination. [. . .] In many ways, the two processes are the same, but the scientist cannot act outside the constraints imposed on him by the world. In this respect, the artist, whether visual artist or the writer or the musician, I think, has the huge advantage, that it is possible to create a great world out of the imagination which has a validity, and in that respect, the scientist is the poorer.

MEREDITH: There's a footnote to that. Auden said that a great artist can be defined as one whose considerable works could only have occurred in the order in which they did occur. And I think it's a very nice touchstone, you can get Verdi up to that level, you can't get a lot of other people that you'd like to.

MacLEAN: Scientists are defined, also, as individuals whose paranoid delusional systems are better organized and documented than those of ordinary people.

GARFINKEL: I would like to go for a moment back to the scientists. I agree with Sir Fred, who said that you can't hold scientists responsible for deciding whether what they discover or what they learn is going to be applied in a positive or a negative way. However, there is a responsibility that I think scientists have as well as the rest of us have, and that is that we develop a scientifically literate population, and I think that there is a diminishment of that in America today, especially at the high school level. Many people who go on to university will take science, but other nations, like Japan and Germany and the Soviet Union, have very strong science and mathematics requirements at their high school level. So if those students ever go to university, they are a highly technical and scientific work force. They make, or they should be able to make, better scientific and technical judgments as a populace, and I think that, for all of the popular science magazines that we might have out today, we don't have a reading public that can make judgments about whether that is, in fact, true or good scientific information, and that, although that may not talk specifically to the interface of science and literature, I think that's a concern that is not being addressed in any educational circles to any degree. I think one of the few places it's being addressed is at the National Science Foundation, and nobody is very willing to listen, and they are a small voice in a very large bureaucracy.

LEFCOWITZ: Does society really want us to play, either as artist or scientist? One wonders if the whole idea of play just seems so unserious, so non-Puritan, that we may have a problem with the audience. On one level they always want to take what we do and turn it into something useful: bombs. On the other level, moral lessons. The dichotomy allows them, on one hand, to damn us because what we've done in play has turned into bombs and, on the other, to damn us because what we have done may turn out to challenge the common morality. So there may be a third force here, which is both us (because of our argument today) but also out in that larger society, which really doesn't know what it wants to do with people who want to play, to come back to Jim's question.

MARCUS: I think that brings to mind something I was thinking of when we were speaking about responsibility and the responsibility scientists have and writers have both to speak out. From society's point of view (people who aren't either scientists or writers), both scientists and writers may seem to have a disproportionate share of influence. We here have been asking, do scientists, from the writer's point of view, have more influence than they ought to and are they all on the wrong side, whichever right or wrong is? And the scientists perhaps think that people who have access to the media, in whatever media, have a disproportionate share of influence. But from outside, both scientists and writers are more intellectually oriented, more educated, and do have better access (or better knowledge of how to get access) to publicizing their views and have had a disproportionate share compared to the rest of the public. The point I want to make is that influence is something that ought to be used carefully. I knew full well when I brought up the point about the Nobel Prize winners on both sides that the Nobel Prize winners who have come out against nuclear power have by and large not been the nuclear scientists. I mention that with this other thought in mind, because sometimes when you're on the opposite side from one of these groups, you say, "Damn it, why do these people get an ear when they really don't know what they're talking about?" You ask, "Why does Jane Fonda get an audience?" if you're not on her side. I think when we want to make our views known and want to do what we think is right, we ought to be aware of the facts and aware of the whole environment of the situation and ought to use our disproportionate power very carefully and very intelligently, because I think sometimes there can be a backlash caused by some of the things we do that none of us would want.

MS. KUMIN: Could you give us an example of the backlash you see here?

MARCUS: I can't think of a particular example off-hand, but I think—well, I think perhaps in many quarters the antinuclear cause has been hurt by people like Jane Fonda, who are not perceived as having any background and who are perceived as using a position where they can get publicity very easily.

MS. KUMIN: That's curious, because I think that, as writers, we feel impotent, and it's curious to hear that there is a misuse of power on the part of public personalities who perhaps are being fed their lines by the writers who feel impotent. As I was sitting here, I could not help but remember the lyrics from a Tom Lehrer song of my generation, "Once the rocket goes up, who cares where it comes down?/That's not my department, said Werner von Braun." And I think that that little couplet represents the extreme sense of impotency that many of us share: that we don't have input into these decisions.

GLASER: I share deeply your commitment, Wendell Berry's commitment. I'm also feeling very confused by that in here, because I think one of the focuses we've taken is our sense of impotence, and not as artists, not as scientists, but as people living in a political environment, and politically, damn it, I am impotent, and I scream at night about it. And yet there's something in what Linda Pastan said that I want to hold on to, and it's a belief that goes back to George Wald. I want to believe that human beings, article of faith, no science, are good. Maybe there even is a God and some ulterior purpose for all of this, and that part of my job as a writer is to write that, my experience of that, and to separate out politics, which I have to become involved in, because I want mankind to continue. And I have to become sharp about it, and I have to be clever and smart and good, but I don't know if it belongs in my writing and I certainly don't know that I can blame anybody for that other than me. And my responsibility is who gets elected, because I really do think that scientists are doing their art like I'm doing my art; where we fail is to recognize the human being underneath the onionskin and that we all bumble about the best we can. What's frightening is that we're bumbling with consequences that we, none of us, understand.

MS. KUMIN: Maybe the discussion should be about that sense of impotence that we share across the table, then scientists and writers.

BARATZ: I've been a resident of the District of Columbia for sixteen years, and there's a rather odd group of people in this city—most of them run the government or influence it. Most of them, at least for the sixteen years that I've been here and for the history of the republic, have not had a vote, so that if you discuss impotence as an issue, a state of mind, a state of personal experience, I ask you in that discussion to judge everything you say against what it feels like to be influenced but not to influence.

LEFCOWITZ: Are we the resistance to the statistical determinism that we at the same time create and believe in?

APPLEMAN: The last several speakers have been giving shape to a feeling that's been growing in the back of my head as we go into the last hour and I'm feeling valedictory about all of this, therefore slightly more frustrated than I was earlier. I suspect a sort of common feeling here now, and I think one of the duties of academics is to think up trouble for other people. Maybe this is the first step, and not a finished process today, of a series of conferences on science and literature to be held somewhere or other. At times we've spoken very effectively, I thought, to each other, and at other times very ineffectively. And I was thinking back to my usual definition of the distinction between a graduate seminar and a dormitory bull session; a good bit of the difference comes from certain shared information and certain focuses in the former that don't exist in the latter. And I thought that perhaps we might give a moment or two to defining the shape of the next conference, and, as possible entries in that series of ideas, I might suggest maybe a dozen, or slightly fewer, scientists of various kinds and a dozen literary people, not only because they're relevant to the work of the group, but because they are also so fiercely interested that they'd even be willing to do some homework. If that were the case, then each person could, say, suggest one substantial essay or one book that would be required reading for such a conference, and to which people could refer with a full understanding, and everyone would instantly understand what that book is about; and that certain key words could be taken out of the transcript of this meeting, some of the words, obviously, that spring to mind immediately, you know, *consciousness, impotence, responsibility,* and so on, and that those words be suggested as motifs, not an agenda, just simply suggestions for motifs for such a conference. And if that were the case, we might get a more disciplined—not that discipline is the only virtue of these things, I think suggestiveness is also very nice, and that's what we've gotten a good bit of in these two days—but a more disciplined discussion of these key ideas and others that are going to grow out of them, that might lead to something that will leave us with a little less sense of frustration next time than we had this time.

PAUL TRACHTMAN (*Smithsonian* magazine): A question. I've detected an enormous gap in some of the discussion between different people who, I think, are trying to say the same things from such different points of view that they're not seeming to communicate. I'm sorry that Wendell Berry is gone, because this is partly about his concern about soil erosion. And yet, he's concerned about the taking of responsibility for our peers in the science community and in literature, and he found the dadaists rather repulsive in seeming not to do that, and that seems to have been a general conception of this. I wonder if O. B. Hardison and perhaps Stephen Baratz, because he has thought about Einstein, would talk a little about this possibility that science and literature both work in metaphors, and that one of the ways of looking at what Einstein was saying with relativity is that you cannot have a thing without an observer. The thing that is described necessarily depends upon how the observer sees it. So it's a process, it's an interaction, and if you remove the observer, there's no description of the thing, there's no possibility of the thing. If that's a correct metaphorical restatement of relativity, that tends to imply to me that there is ethics implicit in that, because the observer is inherently a part of the system, and he has the option to reconceive the thing seen—this'll have to be in Gregg shorthand, because I don't want to make a speech here—essentially, I think the ultimate implications of that are that ideas are potentially machines and that each scientific invention or technology ultimately makes possible some kind of machinery that becomes the objectification of it in the real world, which then affects us, physically, emotionally, and in other ways. Our language doesn't operate that way. The phonetic languages tend to operate so as to create things in their own right, things that exist separately. There are other languages, such as Hopi or the Oriental languages, which don't do that, but we tend to be forced to think of things out there as independent of us, whereas the Einstein revolution says that's not so. And I think that the dadaists were trying to clear the language of that sort of epistemological bind and that they were in some way perceptive about the Einstein change. I don't think that it was an accident that they happened at about the same time or that your paper, O.B., is focusing on that similar period, but that's Picasso and the dadaists there. There's a basis in what Wald and Hardison were saying here for answering Wendell Berry's concern about responsibility. It's sort of an implicit outgrowth of the new cosmology that has emerged in this century. Most of us have not gone back to zero and reconstructed our language. We are not perceptive as to what science is really about now and the kinds of machines that it is unleashing. I don't know if that makes any sense, but I'd like to hear some commentary along those lines, of process rather than thingness.

HARDISON: I would be very reluctant to talk about Einstein and relativity, because I've read a lot of popularized presentations of the material but I'm not at all sure that I understand what it's about. That's why I note the simultaneity of a revolution of the image of nature in physics and the outcropping of new languages in the visual arts and attempts, truncated though they may have been, to discover new ways to use language, or even new languages, for literary expression. As far as the grasp of the world being analogical, I'd say that's universal. And I rest here, very heavily, on the three volumes of Ernst Casirer's *Philosophy of Symbolic Form*, the first of which is devoted to mythology and religion, the second to language, and the third to science, as different symbolic forms for ordering experience and objectifying it and analyzing it. Well, these symbolic forms exist in the mind and they can't be anything else but analogs to relationships in nature. So I think that religion, mythology, literature, and science share a great deal. I've never been very deeply impressed by the two-culture argument; it seems to me to be a false issue rather than a true and deep issue of modern culture. I would say that normally you have a world which is complementary to the symbolic form you carry around in the mind. That's particularly true of the symbolic forms created by your language. As long as culture moves very slowly, your language is going to be complementary to it and can make gradual changes from time to time to accommodate changes in the surrounding culture. But language moves very slowly, and the human psyche changes very slowly once it is formed. What happens if, in a period of fifty years, half of the givens of experience suddenly change? You're going to have a great tension between the culture, which is in one place, and the symbolic forms in your head that are in another place, and you're going to have to try to do something, maybe something pretty desperate, to bring the two back into complementarity. Now, that isn't, I take it, a really great problem in the language of science and mathematics, and that's why I really liked very much Mr. Wald's statement that nature is the solution to the equations of quantum mechanics. But it is a significant problem in the kind of great Rube Goldbergian model of nature which is embodied in the English language and which all of a sudden is no longer as complementary as it used to be with the outside world, and great strains are developing. And I see these efforts radically to transform language to be a response to that, and I see that validated again and again and again in comments like the one of Ponge. I'm tired of the grand old themes; they no longer seem to me to be real, and what we have to do is to get back to the realities of experience and try to embody them in a form that can be communicated, so that other people can objectify them and develop a shared sense of where we are, and some kind of a community can be reestablished.

BARATZ: Since I was mentioned also—as a psychologist, I'm much more interested in what I call social technologies, that is, things that people create to facilitate their interaction. Einstein once detailed, in a letter, the theory of thinking, three-quarters of a page, very short, which turns out to be Gestalt psychology, interestingly enough. And the base of Gestalt psychology is cognition, and the base of cognition is decision processes and information theory. This appropriate social technology turns out to be a state in a democracy in which individuals express their decisions. I think what we see in the emergence of these new linguistic forms is the final convergence in this country of a unified culture. So what I think is happening is that we are coming together, finally, in a process that facilitates decision processes, and that, despite what one may think of government, there is a fairly representative group of citizens in this very city who are gathering to write a constitution which is the ultimate statement of a democracy, the written word, about the nature of the human experience in a cooperative environment. It's my sense that these things kind of collide, and that an enormous amount of the ennui that we are experiencing as a society interestingly enough has its roots in the nonrepresentation of the very large group of people who have had an enormous amount to do with the way in which the government works. It gets back to my statement about impotence, of those who have been basically impotent in the way in which the final decisions have been made. So I don't think I've been very helpful, but, in my mind, the idea of the emergence of new linguistic forms comes about as a result of our searching for commonalities of experience which, in magical ways, basically develop when people form a new state of mind. I might add, parenthetically, that there are three suggestions for the name of the new state, the first one being Columbia, which expresses the dominance, in the scientific community, of NASA in this town. The second is Einstein, which is ditto. And the third is Rainbow. It says something about the people. To me, all of these things make up what I consider to be the imponderability of the nature of communication and its ultimate resolution in the process of decision making, and that's my logic.

LEFCOWITZ: The Indo-European tradition once had a root word for growing, and, possibly with the growth of cities and the neolithic revolution, somebody realized that there was an ontological possibility, not things growing but things being. They took the Indo-European word for grow, and converted it into the word for ontological being. The fun thing is that we no longer had a word for growing, and in that metaphorical process of trying to make our language meet our apprehension—God knows who came up with it—they got a new word, to grow, which was the metaphor for what? Green. To green, which was process, and now we had two distinguishings. One distinction between process and one distinction between some kind of being, and perhaps what the experimenters are doing, as O. B. is pointing out, is exploring once more those metaphors which will let us understand processes of language by which we apprehend our reality. Is this clear?

MEREDITH: I think one of the things that is happening here is that, in the process of talking across a small but real chasm, we have spoken more clearly our thoughts, and it occurs to me that the writers present are all accessible writers; we don't have any Ashbery types, any Mark Strand types; we don't have any Koszinskys. We have only people who are already so defining the work of the writer as to talk to larger elements in the tribe. I think the scientists are probably here because of a similar impulse, and it may be that we can assume that one of the findings of this event, not because of what we have said but because of its being, is that we all feel impelled to talk more plainly to our fellow citizens about the excitements of our work, the provisional optimisms of our work, and about a sense of community. If that's the case then, really, what we're talking about has begun to happen, that we are tired of talking to one another in shop talk, and we'd like to get that kind of usefulness straight, that we are in a tribal society designated to do something for our brothers and sisters, and we're doing it, but we must also be sure that they know we're doing it and that we're doing what they want done. This is more appropriate, I expect, to a writer than it is to a scientist. A scientist has to take the answers that come from the experiments and write them down, and nature is there, possibly not as cozy as the audience of a poet or novelist. What I'm satisfied with is that I've learned a lot about how to listen to a scientist talk, and this is because a scientist has been talking to an ignorant person, essentially. And we've talked about literature at a level that is very nontechnical, but I think the way Wendell Berry talked, particularly, the way John Gardner talks, in a sense, is that we are public servants and we work for the American tribe, or work for a larger tribe, but we are not an élite and we are not alienated.

BEALL: I wanted to second that, though less eloquently. I'm a scientist and I've been involved in public policy. I was a Congressional Fellow for a while, and I don't feel impotent in terms of the abilities of people like people in this room to influence policy decisions that affect all our lives. I think all it takes is time and some inclination to do it, and I think all of us have opportunities every day. I also think that we should not underestimate our influence in a more general way in terms of our connections with people who write and do science. And that in William Meredith's words a sense of community or the sense of tribalness that we ought to have about this can be a very important aspect, a very important influence in terms of those kinds of decisions. Not every one of us has to be involved in public policy directly, but some of us should be, and certainly both writers and scientists, and artists in general, should be involved, in at least part of their careers, in those kinds of decisions and those kinds of activities. So I don't think we should feel quite as impotent as the discussion, until this recent turn of it, seemed to sense. I think we've got a lot of influence. I think all we need to do is use it.

APPLEMAN: It is said the subtitle of every book is "How to Be More Like Me." I think when the world doesn't conform instantly, we're disappointed.

MacLEAN: The thing we really have to be afraid of is this collective mind, it seems to me, and the arrogance of science. I think that turns off a lot of writers, they know everything. They sort of have this compulsion to save the world. I think if people could relax a little more and just realize that human beings are part of nature and everything that they do is natural, then it's nature's fault if things go wrong. But when I get really depressed, that is the thing that comes along and sustains me. At the same time, I'm Aristotelian at heart, and as long as I have two nerve cells to rub together, I just feel this terrible drive and urge to inch upwards a little bit, and one of the things one discovers—you know, investigating the brain gives you great resignation; it stirs you up, too, but it makes you resigned to a lot of things. And the most beautiful thing I've discovered in my lifetime is that the newest part of our brain is tuned in with the most highly evolved part of the early mammalian brain, that is concerned with caring, family, and play. And it's this part of the brain that is looking to the future, always. A concern for self, yes, because if you don't have the empathy to look inward, you can't identify with another individual. And the proudest thing in my whole life is having been identified with the National Institutes of Health, which, more than the World Health Organization, I think, is concerned with human beings and suffering everywhere, and not just animals but plants, too. I mean, this is really sinful to go in and defoliate a country as we have done. And we can trace our ancestry back 250 million years at least, to the Permian times, with the mammal-like reptiles. And this has been a long time, and the few years that are going by now, we just sort of feel as though everything we do is terribly important, but if you look at the mammal-like reptiles, several strains, several lines of them were developing the capacity to hear in parallel, the two little bones of the jaw were becoming smaller and working towards the middle ear. Now, how do you explain that in neo-Darwinian terms? You just can't. And you have a paleontologist, like Olson, who says, "What do we have here? Two systems, one for now, one for the future." And we don't worry enough about some of these other systems that are developing, and who knows but maybe the penguin may be important someday, with that kind of a brain. When the ordinary neuranatomist looks at a bird's brain, he's just like someone who's been put into the cockpit of an airplane and told to fly it; it's just so different. But I've always said if I had to have a brain transplant, I think I'd like a penguin's brain.

PRICE: I'm sure you'll find that penguins are very important to writers, too.

MacLEAN: We just have to confess we don't know where the devil we're going, and we must lose a lot of that arrogance that some scientists have and try to explain everything to everybody. I've just gone through a book and erased all my talking down to the audience, because I think the scientist must be clear, he must make himself plain. But I think he runs into trouble with the most intellectual people in the whole world, and they are the philosophers and the writers and so forth, and scientists got to be where they were because there wasn't anything else left to do. And they're very poor imitators of Einstein, who could hardly learn to tie his shoe. This may be a reptilian brain, it was such a lousy imitating brain that he was just forced by his neocortex to be creative. I think that's a possibility. When I'm not preaching, I try to be humble.

RODDENBERRY: Before we close, I wanted to say a word for the maverick thinkers here. I am personally indebted to everyone here who said anything that made anyone else uncomfortable, as I think that's very important, that one definition of a civilized person is one who is absolutely delighted when someone says, "I disagree with you because . . . ." And I think we should remember that in these conferences.

BEALL: We are all in this together, and I think it's important to remember that.

MILLER: I'd like to say a few things about the kind of person who moves from one field to the other. We have not talked very much about that, and since Dr. Appleman is concerned with our taking away homework assignments, I could suggest four distinguished writers that I know who began as engineers and came over into writing, and all of them tell me that they don't really feel that they've moved from one field to the other, that they essentially feel that the training in engineering was good for them in literature. Let me just give you the examples. Among poets, I would say, Michael Heller and Hugh Seidman are both splendid poets and people that we should be looking at very carefully, everybody in the room, and yet they began as engineers and don't regret it a bit. Certainly one of our most innovative and promising writers is Ken Gangemi, who started out as an engineer, served a long time in the Air Force as a pilot, and is now a writer who will turn to any form simply because, as an engineer, he thinks first in terms of function and then designs. And so he's likely to wind up with anything from a poem, a new kind of poem to a new kind of novel. But I guess the best example is Kurt Vonnegut, who not only is grateful that he started out as a mechanical engineer, which he describes as "slow physics," but says that he's a good writer, if he's a good writer at all, simply because he came into it from a totally different field and is a total naif and can look at literary problems as though they had no history. From the other direction, I'd say, of course, Doris Lessing, who's been mentioned here many times before, because, as she goes from *The Golden Notebook* to *Shikasta*, she's going from a novel in which the main problem is Why does art always miscarry?, in *The Golden Notebook*, to *Shikasta*, where she feels that if she's going to reach a wide audience, she's got to write science fiction.

ACKERMAN: About this book list, I wonder if it would be out of line to suggest that, when we go home, we collaborate on a bibliography and then circulate it among ourselves as a sort of interdisciplinary chain letter.

BEALL: An excellent idea. I would also, in reference—

BRODERICK: This would be, send 5 names and in thirty days you'll get 125.

BEALL: We're almost at the closing point here. What I would like to do is, because there are such diverse interests, go around and have people briefly state what they hoped to get from the conference or what they would like to see discussed in possible future conferences or what they think the issues are that we need to address. And I would caution you that we have little time and many people, so if you will make your statements brief, we will try that.

ANN KELLY: I think that in future conferences, it might be better to focus on a single narrow issue, such as the use of science as a source of imagery for the poet or writer, or the topic you suggested, which was people who had gone from one field to another. I think, in a way, we've been going off in various directions, and although it's been very stimulating in many ways, it's very frustrating, too, because the conversation doesn't evolve toward some sense of depth.

MARSHALL: One thing I'd like to see happen is to have this type of symposium and see the results of it have an effect in and of themselves. And perhaps at the next one I'd like there to be educators present who are involved in the formulation of curricula and so forth so that the whole business of creative process and inculcating it in children taking an active part in their own learning, instilling a lifelong curiosity and that sort of thing. I teach in Poets-in-the-Schools, and I do my work in the classroom from the point of view that you can teach certain precepts of creative process that are applicable to any discipline, science or language arts, and that it's going against the grain of the delivered body of knowledge, which was my experience in learning science and in learning literature as a child, and I'm trying to work against what I feel is a rather deadening, passive kind of education. . . .

LAD: I should like to have scientists talk about what they actually do; writers, too, how science infringed on their work; a meeting ground might emerge. . . .

PRICE: This is the first of these conferences I've experienced . . . . There are many issues. Perhaps we should focus a little more in the next one on literature and science. My expectation, when I came to this, was that we would be hearing from scientists who were also writers and vice versa, and I'm not sure I've heard enough of that topic that I would like to hear. And so, hopefully, as we get involved in future conferences, we'll all experience more of that.

HOYLE: Well, as an outsider here, it did occur to me from time to time, when I was listening to the discussion, that it might have been an advantage to have had a creative musician or a creative artist at times. I don't know if that's allowed by your rules, but it did seem to me—perhaps I'm saying the wrong thing. Before I stop, there's just a word about science that I wonder if I could have: I got the impression that there was a sort of feeling that science is a known body of facts and of theory. It isn't really quite like that. I think one should think of science as a very broad spectrum where, at one end of the spectrum, what is known is essentially certain. I've talked about twenty-decimal-place accuracy; it might even be more than that at one end of the spectrum. At the other end of the spectrum, the situation is quite uncertain. And there are all grades between these two possibilities, and the people who are doing research are trying to hit the place in that spectrum where they consider the most sensitive margin between what is known and what is not known, that's what one is always trying to do in research. Now, I would agree with what has just been said, in the sense that scientists do tend to be too arrogant, they tend to weight the spectrum towards what is known. I find this constantly, in arguing with my colleagues, that they will believe that they know for certain something which really belongs to the center part of the spectrum, where there is genuine uncertainty. I think we heard a remark about Darwinian evolution. I would very much agree with that remark; I think there's much more there that's uncertain than biologists tend to believe. But it is a very broad issue. One should neither think that because scientists make mistakes, that it's all wrong—there is a section that really is very, very solid—there are other parts that are very uncertain.

MARCUS: I think I share the sense of several other people that this meeting has been very broad-ranging and has taken us over a large number of topics, any one of which we could have profitably looked at in greater depth, and perhaps this was very useful as a first meeting to bring to the surface what all the topics were. An area in which we might well go into greater depth relates to the need for scientific literacy, and I'm not quite sure what the opposite wording is, but the need for scientists to be literate, I guess. I think the comment made about the scientific literacy of our general populace, which includes writers and everyone else who's not trained in science, versus that of other countries is a very important public policy issue today. I think the opposing issue, of scientists who have a great deal of influence in the world and maybe, in some peoples' view, have less concern or less of a philosophical background, to apply what they learn and help in applying it to the public. There's probably a need for exploring the needs in training scientists outside of their areas of science. That would be possibly a profitable topic for another meeting.

MILLER: If I should pick new areas, I think there would be two. I'd like to see much more exploration of the way in which patterns of creativity are similar in both fields. At the same time, I'd like to point out that Wald's speech included much more literature than people seemed to think. I heard a lot of comments on the way out about how there was a lot of science but no literature, but all that mythology was literature, and he was constantly relying on mythology to make some of his points. The other question I would like to hear discussed in the future is: to what extent are the values of both science and literature stultified by their shotgun marriages to the profit system?

MacLEAN: I was interested in Phil Appleman's mention of a dozen individuals, because that's about the average number of a social group of mammals. When you get into larger groups, that thirteen number seems to have something ominous about it, and when you take a collection of reptilian children and put them in groups of a hundred or two hundred, boy, you've got something to deal with, and I think that's where curiosity begins to go down the drain, that's when you just chop off the head. So that would be interesting to experiment with, I would say, Phil.

BARATZ: I think the next meeting ought to take up the challenge that O. B. Hardison put to this meeting, which is to figure out what happened in 1895 to 1910.

RODDENBERRY: I enjoyed this thoroughly; this was my first time, I'm not disappointed in any part of it. About the only slight criticism I might make is—and something I hesitated over—is whether, maybe, science and literature and so on is perhaps defined a bit too narrowly and not keeping up with where our world is rushing so headlong at the present time.

HARDISON: I have to say that I imagined many meetings during the weekend before this would start, and this was better than anything that I could possibly have imagined, so I am very pleased with it. I do have one request to the scientists in the group, and that is, before the next meeting, please invent a cure for the common cold.

SELTZER: I very much enjoyed this, and, while I agree it would help to have more focus, I hope that the organization would work it so we would also get this wide diversity. Maybe a combination of smaller sessions that have specific topics that people might either choose or be arbitrarily thrown together in to get that diversity of views, and then occasional general sessions, where everybody could get involved and then throw out the issues that were most important in the smaller sessions. . . .

SARGENT: I don't have anything earth-shaking to propose. I enjoyed the conference; I think it was a happy thought to assemble a group of scientists and poets and writers in the same room and sit across a table and bullshit, and as long as it's reasonably administered and people have a chance to talk, I think almost anything would work. It depends on the individuals who get invited.

ALENIER: I guess I'm always looking for new vehicles of communications, and I live in a number of different worlds with different kinds of communications, whether it's writing poetry or doing computer work or any of the other kinds of arts things that I like to do, dance, and just museum-going, and I think that the diversity here was a definite plus, and that, by narrowing to a certain group, which we did and didn't do, I think that there was a benefit, that there wasn't a one-sided picture presented here.

GALBRAITH: I've been thrilled to be part of the Library where this took place, and I'm going to pass on making any suggestions until I assimilate some of what's been said here. I've loved it.

ACKERMAN: Well, after all of these terrific suggestions, this is a little bit like that game, "I'm going to the seashore and I'm going to take with me. . . ." I like all of these suggestions, but also, I hope at the next meeting the issues would be known ahead of time, so we could really focus our thoughts, especially those of us who find it easier to think on paper. And also, I'd so much be interested in a discussion of what intellectual and creative processes scientists and artists have in common, whether the creative act is the same as it occurs in both disciplines. I've come away from this meeting with a sense that what we share is the affectionate curiosity of naturalists for the world. I think that's a very powerful collusion against the state of society that we've been finding so dismaying this afternoon, and is in itself worth getting together again for.

LEFCOWITZ: I probably got the most immediate practical use of anybody out of this conference, because I'll be teaching a course in science and literature at the Naval Academy. I'd like to see, for the next conference, as one of the topics, something relating to the formal impact of technology and science on literature. O. B., in a way, in his paper, I think, started to deal with it. This may, in fact, have to deal in part with the reeducation of our audience. You can't start tearing newspapers until you have the technology of cheap newsprint. The impact of photography on, for example, the shifts in modern art. Maybe the impact on plot formation, for those of us who are fiction writers, because of changes both in the audience and technological change. The impact on poetry of literal kinds of shifts in technology, recognition of the very nature of print, the move from the oral to the visual, and maybe vice versa. In short, the degree to which the interests of literature, which I think, to a large extent, still control the education system, need to be considered in terms of the shaping of the activities that the scientist, perhaps subliminally—I'm not saying this well—the shape of their scientific activities by the kind of education they're getting from the age of five until twenty-one through an educational system largely still controlled by humanities formed in the medieval period.

POURNELLE: I will start with an apology. I tend to be very loud because I have not heard my own voice since the Korean War, and for that I simply apologize. I do not know how loud I talk because I was in artillery duel for a very long time, and after that the speech frequencies are pretty well gone in my ears, and I have no bone-conductive hearing. My wife steps on my foot when I shout at people, but there was no one here kind enough to do that for me. Secondly, I sometimes think that writers probably should not be allowed to present themselves in public, anyway. I spend a great part of my life alone in a room with the door closed, accompanied only by characters of my own creation who are not very tractable; they insist on doing things that I don't want them to do, but at least I have some control over them in that when they insult me I can insult them back without too much difficulty. And I often think I became a writer because my relatives kept interrupting me at the dinner table, and if you're a writer, no one can. And I'm not at all convinced that the writers' conferences really work in the sense that I don't know of anyone who's a successful writer who isn't a fairly colossal egotist. To begin with, I'm not sure you can do it. But if you will concede that putting such cantankerous people into a situation of academics, which this sort of is, and if you will concede that's interesting, then this has certainly been interesting. It certainly was for me. I met Mr. Berry, whom I have argued with in correspondence for some time, and discovered him to be about as delightfully cantankerous as I thought he was going to be when I met him, and I find he has much the same view of me. We both think we are irascible sons-of-bitches, but at least we now know what we each look like. I will make the second piece of my apologia by saying that I was encouraged, both last night and at lunch today, to say more, on the grounds that, like Sir Fred and a couple of others, I am, in fact, both, having made some contributions to science in the human factors business, and whether or not what I write is literature I don't know, but I have, in fact, won a couple of awards for my *succés d'estime*, as well as having written some best-sellers, which pay the bills, and I also have audited the books of a major publisher, and am probably the only person you know who made a publisher pay out a million dollars to his writers, which I did, and it took a lot of my time. So I do know something about the publishing business, and I was encouraged to say things, so I apologize, madam, for being noisy, but there was some encouragement. For the future, I think there probably should be a few more spokespersons for what I would call, in this room, unpopular views, but when you get outside and downtown, would be what I would call fairly popular views. That is to say that whether or not the majority culture is contemptible is in my judgment not a closed subject. And I do not concede that there are no enemies to the left, that the intelligentsia must automatically have a certain social philosophy, that it must, in fact, be automatically alienated. And I may be the only Republican in this room. And yet that is certainly not a totally contemptible intellectual position. I have got to it through a very circuitous route that includes having been a state committeeman for the Communist party as an undergraduate, and, for the improvement of the thing in future, I really think you ought to have a couple of articulate people like Milton Friedman or someone. I don't concede that Reaganomics, supply-side economics, is on a par with dadaist babbling, which you put forth in your paper as if this equation were something that we were just automatically to believe. Well, I believe that it is at least defensible that that's not true. I think a number of things have been said here as if they are jokes to be laughed at, and I think the opposite is defensible. It may not be true, it may well be that the economic system of the present administration is stupid, but I do not believe it is concedable in advance without at least a little discussion. And I do not think that the intellectuals and the intelligentsia must inevitably be alienated. I do not believe that the Erich Fromm position and the Herbert Marcuse position—I think none of us really understand what Marcuse thought he was saying— I do not believe those ought to be automatically conceded without some debate. And if I were to try to suggest how to improve this discussion, I would say you probably ought to have a couple more irascible sons-of-bitches on my side of the aisle as well as a couple more of them on Wendell Berry's side, and that would be a lot more fun.

LEFFLER: I'm not sure I can follow Jerry up very well. It's kind of interesting that one of the things that's been bandied about has been the arrogance of scientists, the arrogance of science. And listening to Sir Fred, Dr. MacLean, Professor Wald, of course, Mr. Kumin, I haven't heard very much arrogance at all. In fact, there's been quite a good deal of humility, and so in one way I would agree with Jerry, I would like to see some arrogant scientists, not necessarily politicians, but scientists who might respond in a way that we haven't heard some of these scientists respond. I don't know if it's a matter of age or long terms of investigation of science, but one of the curious things to me, having been a person who was educated as a physicist and then worked as an engineer and then thought that I was leaving to teach literature and write poems, I find myself having come back, not to becoming an engineer again—I could never do that—but reading more and more in physics, particularly, more recently in biology. I'm not simply looking for metaphors, I'm reading because one of the things that science seems to confirm over and over and over again is a sense of mystery, a sense that the more we go, the more that horizon seems to recede. And I think that's evident in what some of the scientists have said here today, have evoked in the nature of their language: this sense of humility, which is a kind of paradox, to some degree, because as we've talked about, science seemed to become so dominant, so alienating, as the eighteenth century wore on into the nineteenth century, and poets and writers were alienated from science. It seems we're coming through another circle again, leading us back, in some degree (at least in the study of physics, in molecular biochemistry), to a certain sense of humility, and I think that would be an interesting issue to investigate. Another one has to do with science and technology. I do not think it is possible to separate out science and technology. On the other hand, I think that anybody who writes anything is using science, science being a matter of knowledge, a matter of investigation. Science is contributing to our knowledge, it alters our means of understanding; by altering our means of understanding it alters the language; by altering the language, we alter our perceptions. And so, therefore, we're all using science. Whether we write, or are opposed to science, so-called, are opposed to technology, that's another issue. I think that depends on the individual writer. But all of us are using that extension of human knowledge which is reflected in our language, which is continually changing. And I'm not sure we've really made those distinctions. It's a distinction that, I think, was brought up when we first met back in 1979, and I think that's one of the values, and it's something that we talked about then, but it's been brought up over again as we've gone around the table, about trying to set out specific issues, issues that at least would provide some gravitational center that could at least bring us back. So I'm seconding that idea that we choose some specific issues and maybe examples. We've been talking in the most abstract ways, and I think it has put me into a certain kind of silence, because it's much easier to discuss specific things. Maybe it's that notion of Ezra Pound's in the back of my mind where he said, "Go in fear of abstractions; we can become captured by them and mesmerized by them." There is something about talking about things in the concrete and then generalizing from the concrete, and I think we've been going off in the opposite direction, speaking about these enormous abstractions, and it's hard to grab hold.

APPLEMAN: This follows pretty well from Merrill's comment. I felt that frequently we, at least the writers, were being appropriately tough on the scientists, but I didn't feel any corresponding toughness. I think we were too soft on the writers, and I would like to see a conference in which literature is held more to account, because—although I agree completely with Linda Pastan that a writer has his own internal integrity to promote first of all, and I agree with Mr. Roddenberry that I would be offended if someone came in and said that tomorrow you write a play about the five-year plan for producing wheat; I don't believe in those kinds of superimposed responsibility. Nevertheless, literature does engage the world at some level, and the level at which it engages the world, at which it is informed and socially well-intentioned and so on, is important, I think, to the world, to society, but not necessarily to literature. It may be, in some cases, counterproductive to literature, but in some cases it works well as literature and in many cases it works well for society. And I would like to feel that literature didn't constantly get lost in the shuffle as we discuss these issues precluded by, superimposed upon by, ideas that are really social ideas or philosophical ideas or something that are wonderful ideas but not literary. I mean, if we're going to talk about that, we should call it something else at another conference.

PASTAN: I guess I'd like to see a breaking down of barriers of various sorts and perhaps more sharing. I very much liked Pramod's idea that all the writers take three or four minutes to read a poem or a story and the scientists discuss their work a little bit. Perhaps there could be one forum open to the public, where there was not a reading, but there was maybe twelve people up on the stage talking about these issues that a general audience from the area could be invited to listen to. In the spirit of play that O. B. kept talking about, and Mr. Wald, maybe there should be a half an hour in which we ask the scientists to write a poem and the poets to solve an equation. Finally, for those who think that the barriers are insurmountable, I just wanted to say that I'm a poet and my husband is a molecular biologist, and I'd like to think that we're a metaphor for the fact that a marriage between science and poetry really is possible.

GLASER: How long have you been married?

PASTAN: Twenty-eight years.

GLASER: I've enjoyed today. I didn't expect that we'd arrive at any answers and I don't know that we have, which is probably good. I think I've formulated some clear questions for myself, and I'm excited about pursuing those in the privacy of my own room for awhile. One question that I want to spend time on is wondering about the dualism, the dichotomy and yet compatibility, of language and experience that is very abstract, and our desire to be very precise also. And I think that we have a desire that's as old as Adam to name the names of things, and that asks for a kind of precision which is in both writing and in science; and yet our world, in many ways, expresses itself more and more abstractly, so that it becomes harder and harder to name those things that are part of our experience. And I'm excited about thinking about that, and I thank you all for sharing yourselves. It's been a grand experience.

SKLAREW: Just sitting in this room, I have the feeling that we have the potential to enchant one another. For example, I would like to have us hear how Jim Beall sees the night sky and how Paul MacLean sees our brains—I could go around the room—and so, I feel hungry for something that didn't quite happen. And so, I agree with Pramod and Linda that I think that there must be some way that we could keep away from issues and doctrines which we need only to cross the street to get a fill of, if we're hungry for that, and begin specifically and with a specific vision for each of us of what it is we do. Moreover, what we do, not even a vision of it, just to say something about what we do. And I believe in play, we've created a two-day space, and it would be good to have more play and less doctrine, and for that I would get myself a penguin brain like Dr. MacLean.

MR. KUMIN: Well, I guess I'm very defensive or somewhat proprietary about my peers, and if I count correctly, there were nine scientists or technologists and thirty-one writers here, and unless we assume that the intellectual weight of the scientists is three times the intellectual weight of the writers, there's an imbalance. The count may be wrong, because there probably are a lot of closet scientists among the writers that were never announced. But I think in a future meeting, there really ought to be a better balance, there really ought to be more—if we're going to have a dialogue, we can't have writers having a dialogue among themselves, we have to have more scientists present. I think it would be useful to make a language understandable to the scientists, to have, as Linda Pastan suggested, at least a smattering of a public audience so we can keep ourselves honest with the language that we're using to communicate. Other than that, I think that the conference has been very useful and I hope it will go on and I hope that its output will be somehow communicated to the world out there, where it needs to be heard.

MEREDITH: I made my statement before I was asked to.

MS. KUMIN: I'm also going to pass, because I'm going to start to redress the balance that Victor spoke of already, since, like Linda Pastan, I am one-half of a poet-and-scientist combo. I think that I'll let it stand. We so seldom get a chance to be on the same team that I'm speechless. I think this has been wonderful; I would like to see it happen again.

BEALL: I think that you all have spoken very eloquently about a future conference. This has been an interesting session for me; I've been delighted by your participation, and I am pleased to have been able to be here among such company.

BRODERICK: Perhaps I should respond to a few of the suggestions. On the idea of a second conference, this is not out of the question, and we will certainly take the suggestions that have been made quite seriously. I suppose I'm responsible for most of the things people have objected to, the number, for example, and the absence of an audience. We've had a number of conferences here at the Library of Congress and in years past we have had them in the Coolidge Auditorium where we had the readings last night, with an audience. That involved, in my estimation, too great a separation and, I suppose I would say, too much posturing on the stage and too little sense of participation from the audience. Our intent in this conference was to do something to reverse those kinds of imbalances. As for Victor's point, we did, of course, want to have a better balance. You know, however, you invite people to a conference and the demography of the conference is bound by the acceptances. Perhaps writers have more time to come to conferences than scientists. I was very interested in the fact that a number of people that were referred to as possible useful additions to the conference were invited: Chandrasekar, for example, who is a member of our Council of Scholars here at the Library of Congress. He and his colleagues on the Council of Scholars last year, in the first symposium of that body, discussed the subject of creativity and brought up these biographical studies that he had made in some of the discussion. We will be publishing the results of that conference, or the first results of that conference, not the papers themselves, but a pamphlet on creativity, which we regard as the first in what we're calling an inventory of knowledge. Essentially, it's about a dozen problems in the investigation of creativity. And, for one thing, we'll send a copy to each one of you of that at publication. Someone asked me yesterday what the Library expected to accomplish by holding this conference, and I didn't answer then, but I'll answer now that I think that we proposed to accomplish what has been accomplished. If nature is the solution of the quantum equations, maybe this is the solution of our premises. We had no axe to grind, merely an opportunity to give a forum for the exchange of ideas, and I think that the exchange has been lively and broad-ranging, and perhaps some of the things that have been suggested, for example, we did consider, especially when Bob Hayden and I first talked about this conference. It was going to be slightly different from the one we have now, but maybe we should be moving toward that other conference. We've just about used up our time; Maxine said earlier that we would all go out in an apocalypse. If the name of the Library bus is "Apocalypse," it's waiting for you down in the parking lot, and, until we meet again, thank you for coming.

APPENDIX

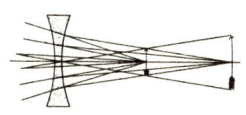

The Poetry of Nothing
O. B. HARDISON

> The artist is a human being like the rest of us. He cannot solve these problems [of modern life] except as one of us; but through his art he can help us see and understand them, for artists are the sensitive antennae of society.
>
> —Alfred H. Barr, Jr., *What is Modern Painting?*

The essay that follows is an excerpt from a longer work on the nature of identity in technological culture. The essay examines a paradox that is evident in certain kinds of twentieth-century poetry. The paradox is that, although the poetry in question is presented in natural languages or apparent derivations from natural languages, it seems to reject the function for which natural languages exist, the communication of meaning. It is, in the phrase used for the title of this essay, a poetry of nothing.

To many people, the poetry I will be discussing seems bizarre, flippant, or even insulting. I will therefore begin with an attempt to place it in the context of other, related aspects of twentieth-century culture and will close with a few suggestions about its larger significance.

The quotation from Alfred Barr's *What is Modern Painting?* that begins this essay asserts that the function of art is to help us "see and understand" the problems of modern life. Since Barr is dealing with visual art, he uses the verb *see* literally as well as in the figurative sense illustrated by the sentence, "I see what you mean."

His assertion appears to be a tautology. "I see what you mean" is normally identical with "I understand what you mean." There is an important sense, however, in which Barr's sentence is not a tautology. Seeing is perceptual and understanding is cognitive. The seeing that art makes possible, whether the art is visual or verbal, is of a specific moment in the spiritual life of the artist. The moment includes both interior and exterior elements that are fused in the unity of consciousness. The exterior elements are not simply things and the interior elements are not simply emotions. Every experience is the product of both. Each experience is subjective in the sense that it can only occur in the consciousness of the person who has it; but it is objective in the sense that it can legitimately be called an objectification in the mind of the data the mind has synthesized. The experience becomes objective in the common sense of the term—that is, in the sense of being publicly available—when it is expressed in a medium such as musical notes or paint or words on a page. The medium allows it to be communicated to others.

To communicate effectively the artist needs talent, but he also draws on languages—whether verbal or visual or musical—that are appropriate to his purpose. For the most part, such languages are available ready-made from tradition. They need only be creatively adapted to the special circumstances of the experience to be communicated. On the other hand, if the available languages are out of phase with what the artist has experienced, his task becomes extremely difficult. He must, in effect, invent a new language or remain silent. In "Language and Logic" Benjamin Lee Whorf describes this problem as it relates to the new physics of the early twentieth century:

> Modern thinkers have long since pointed out that the so-called mechanistic way of thinking has come to an impasse before the great frontier problems of science. To rid ourselves of this way of thinking is exceedingly difficult when we have no linguistic experience of any other, and when our most advanced logicians and mathematicians do not provide any other—and obviously they cannot without the linguistic experience. In the mechanistic way of thinking is perhaps just a type of syntax natural to Mr. Everyman's daily use of the western Indo-European languages, rigidified and intensified by Aristotle and the latter's medieval and modern followers.

Once an art work has been created, there are two ways of understanding it. The first is the sharing or appreciation of the work. The second is the critical understanding that results from formal analysis. The first type of understanding, the sharing, is absolute. If we appreciate a work of art, we appreciate it whether or not we can explain why. In fact, many people resent being asked to explain why, a point illustrated by the familiar complaint, "We murder to dissect." The second type of understanding, the analytic, is not absolute. Its validity depends on theories and methods that are contingent. Since no one is omniscient, theories and methods are necessarily contingent. Criticism can never provide definitive answers to the questions it asks, only the best answers possible given the state of the art of criticism at the time the answers are sought.

To say that a work of art helps us "see and understand" contemporary experience is to say that it helps us understand experience in the absolute sense of sharing and in the contingent sense of providing objects of analysis that lead to probable conclusions. The difference between the two kinds of seeing is the difference between reading a novel or watching a television drama for enjoyment and subjecting the novel or drama to critical analysis to find out why it is effective or what it has to say about things that interest us, like psychology or ethics or economics or history or basket weaving.

Because art begins in the consciousness of a particular artist at a particular moment in time, works of art differ from one another. Works of art from the same culture and same period of history tend to share underlying characteristics that can be summed up as a period style. The similarities of works of art by the same artist constitute a personal style.

A final but important point is that a work of art can be a valid expression of experience whether or not the artist is fully conscious of the elements being objectified. For the most part, artists are *not* conscious of all of the elements they express in their work. Dramatists were excellent psychologists long before Sigmund Freud, and musicians did very well for centuries even though they had little or no knowledge of acoustics. Art is not created by specialists in specific areas of knowledge but by artists. When Hart Crane wrote his great poem "The Brooklyn Bridge," he made no pretense of understanding the high technology that allowed John Augustus Roebling to create the structure. The poem is nevertheless a useful source of information about the human significance of Roebling's technology. Occasionally, of course, the artist does draw on specialized knowledge, including scientific knowledge. One thinks of Leonardo's knowledge of anatomy, of Alexander Pope's use of Newton in his *Essay on Man*, of Audubon's paintings of birds, of Eugene O'Neill's debt to Freud in his *Mourning Becomes Electra* trilogy.

Modern art emerged with stunning suddenness in Western culture between 1890 and 1915. Various antecedents of the modernist movement in art can be found much earlier than 1890, but they can only be recognized as such in retrospect, which is to say that they seemed at the time of their appearance to be variations on accepted norms or eccentric deviations from those norms. What happened between 1890 and 1915 defined a new norm which modern culture is still struggling to understand.

If art expresses states of consciousness, the new art expresses a new state of consciousness. This new state of consciousness was manifested at first in the work of a small number of individuals working in quite different media. Apparently, these individuals were especially sensitive to changes that had been occurring in the culture around them. Their sensitivity is reflected in the radical break which they made with prior traditions. In effect, they came to realize that the languages they had inherited were inadequate to the reality they were experiencing, and they were forced to invent new languages.

That a radical cultural change of some sort took place in the early twentieth century is commonplace. Frequently this change is associated with the First World War, a position illustrated in Paul Fussell's brilliant *The Great War and Modern Memory*. The First World War was unquestionably a cultural watershed. The change that it publicized had, however, occurred before it began. The war was not a cause of change so much as an exposure of the inadequacy of traditional values and a demonstration in the most sensational possible terms of how far the change had progressed.

The change can be traced in many areas of culture. It is especially dramatic in three: science, visual art, and literature.

Freud's *Interpretation of Dreams*, published in 1900, was part of the change. However, the decisive change in science occurred in physics rather than psychology. It was the work of such figures as Maxwell, Rutherford, Planck, Bohr, and Einstein. It can be dated symbolically by the publication date (1905) of Einstein's papers on special relativity, mass-energy equivalence, Brownian motion, and the photon theory of light. The moment was decisive because after it, the time-honored mechanistic view of Nature was no longer tenable. The external world was still there, but it had lost its comforting solidity and uniformity. In fact, relativity had far more radical implications than the introduction of heliocentric astronomy in the Renaissance. If the heliocentric system undermined time-honored religious beliefs, it also vindicated the power of human reason and the rationality of Nature. Relativity, conversely, appeared to set limits to rational knowledge and to unsettle Nature herself. It was as though mankind had been lifted out of a secure two-bedroom house and dropped without warning into the hall of mirrors of an amusement park. Einstein's theory was ridiculed, misrepresented, and ignored, even by some scientists, but for those who understood Einstein, it was the beginning of a new era, and, as Whorf points out, demanded new modes of thought and a new language to express them.

In the visual arts a different sort of change was occurring. It is reflected in the movement in painting and sculpture from representation to abstraction. The movement was foreshadowed by the construction of the Eiffel Tower for the Paris Exposition of 1889. The Eiffel Tower is a pure form. It makes no bow to past history through fluted columns or pointed arches or statues in niches. Its form expresses nothing but its technology, and in this respect it looks forward to the work of the Bauhaus after World War I. The statement made by the Eiffel Tower, however, was ambiguous because the Eiffel Tower did not insist on being regarded as a work of art. It could be dismissed as an overgrown gadget, a curious, picturesque landmark against which tourists liked to be photographed.

If we are concerned with a change of consciousness in art rather than a change of the culture that surrounded the artists, the best symbolic date is 1907, the date of Picasso's *Les Damoiselles d'Avignon*. This painting is not quasi-art like the Eiffel Tower, but explicitly and self-consciously high art. It demands to be seen as well as noticed. What it states when it *is* seen is that art has discovered a new language. The message was obviously timely. Picasso was soon joined by a group of artists that included Kandinsky, Marinetti, Braque, Duchamp, Brancusi, and Mondrian, among many others.

Each of the avant garde artists of the early twentieth century had a unique personality and a unique style. Most of them influenced each other; a few acted as independently, apparently, as Newton and Leibniz in the discovery of calculus. When the artists cited influences outside of the world of painting that affected their work, they ranged across the whole landscape of their culture: primitive African and Iberian art, disgust with Philistinism, hatred of class oppression, Einstein's relativity, Freud's psychology, industrial technology, and more. All of these influences were undoubtedly operative. They were symptoms of radical cultural change, and they intensified the pressure on traditional forms of consciousness. In retrospect, however, it appears that the chief influences on the new art came from within the world of art itself, just as the chief influences on the creation of the new physics came from physics. While physics was creating a new scientific language, art was thus, more or less simultaneously and independently, creating a new visual language.

While Whorf's observation that the new physics requires a new language is very much to the point, it should not be taken to mean that one can discover simple correlations between the languages of modern science and the languages of modern art. It does, however, point to the general tendencies which the new languages share. In becoming abstract, modern painting rejected the traditional and personal elements that had characterized Western art from the Renaissance to the nineteenth century. In theory, a perfectly abstract painting can be as free of tradition and personality, if it wants to, as a circle or a triangle or a randomly curving line. Indeed, modern art has sometimes consciously used randomness to break away from the traditional and personal associations that the artist carries in his subconscious, as, for example, the aleatory music of John Cage, the paintings of Jackson Pollock, and both computer music and computer drawing.

The corollary of abstraction is universality. A painting of a scene like "The Rest on the Flight from Egypt," for example, is immediately recognizable—hence transparent—to a Western European but opaque to a viewer who is not familiar with the Bible; while a Chinese calligraphic painting is opaque to Western viewers, who cannot read the words, although they may admire the flow of the lines. Because abstract art is, in this sense, not the property of a single artist or nation or culture, it is, like geometry, everyone's property. If it comments on anything, it comments on the way perception is shaped by the world; and if it imitates anything, it imitates the forms and categories of spiritual life.

In literary history Baudelaire, Verlaine, and Rimbaud occupy a place roughly analogous to the impressionists in painting. A possible symbolic date for the appearance of a new form of literary consciousness in Western culture is 1897, the date of the publication of Stephan Mallarmé's poem "Un Coup de Dés"—"A Throw of the Dice."

"Un Coup de Dés" is by no means as radical a break with the past as the Eiffel Tower. It is quite radical, however, in relation to literary tradition, which tends to be more conservative than technology if only because it is oriented toward natural language, which is innately conservative. The poem is the culmination of a theme that is present in many of Mallarmé's earlier works and may be labeled "the difficulty of writing." In enacting this theme on the page it becomes the record of an intense struggle to overcome silence—to discover a poetic language capable of expressing the reality of a world ruled by chance and ordered only by arbitrary acts of the mind.

Mallarmé's solution is a language that is fragmented and kaleidoscopic. The moods that his language evokes change so rapidly that they can hardly be glimpsed before they dissolve. But the words are only part of the expression. The pages (and in editions that conscientiously follow Mallarmé's printing instructions, units of two pages) become part of the expression rather than a neutral ground for the black letters formed by the type. Words are sometimes written sequentially, sometimes arranged in falling order, and sometimes separated by page-sized blank spaces. Lines are printed in headline type, in small capitals, in lower-case, and in both headline and small italics (fig. 1). On the last two-page unit a reference to a constellation is reinforced by a word arrangement that echoes the shape of Ursa Major. The poem thus looks forward to the experiments of dada with randomness and the experiments of concrete poets with forms of expression that are visual as well as verbal.

The subject of the poem is randomness, a throw of the dice. The world has no meaning, but the mind endlessly imposes order on it by arbitrary acts much like throws of dice. The blank expanse of the page becomes a visual representation of the sea. Meaning is created on the page by the progression of the words which literally express the victory of the poet over silence, and in the poem by the idea of a journey, even though it is probably a trip to nowhere. The poet struggles for meaning, falls back exhausted, and then begins the struggle again. Near the end of the poem there is a constellation—a destination—but it is in-

Fig. 1. Pages 1 and 2 of Mallarmé's **Un Coup de Dés**. Note the similarity to Breton's dada poem (fig. 2).

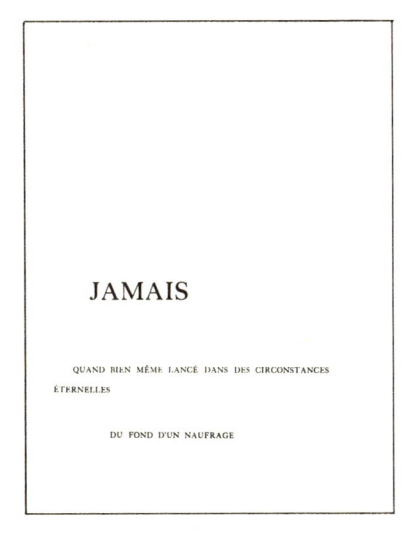

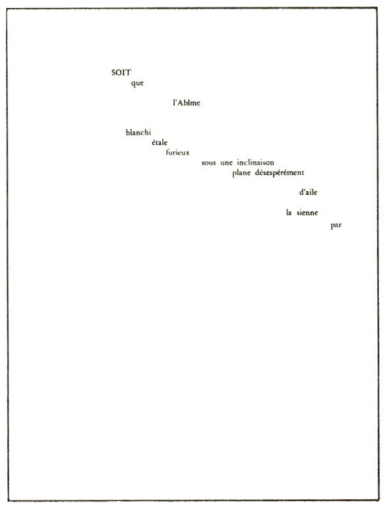

finitely distant, perhaps a myth. Beginning with the title, the phrases in capitals march through several pages like a dominant voice: "A THROW OF THE DICE . . . NEVER . . . WILL ELIMINATE . . . CHANCE." The poem ends on the same note: "Tout Pensée émet un Coup de Dés.": "All thought causes a throw of the dice."

The search of twentieth-century poets for verbal languages adequate to experience is as fascinating and as complicated as the search of painters for new visual languages. In three literary movements the search moves beyond the point defined by Mallarmé's "Un Coup de Dés" to extremes that are something like abstraction in art.

These movements are dada, concrete poetry, and algorithmic poetry. They are related by a common tendency to treat natural language as a potentially transparent, hence universal, medium. Since all natural languages are geographically localized and historically conditioned in their phonetics, lexical meanings, grammars, and literary forms, the tendency seems to distort language in ways that do not apply to painting, sculpture, dance, and music. Unlike these media, language is supposed to convey meaning. When it is pushed by various strategies toward transparency, it loses its capacity to convey meaning as that term is usually understood. The language is new but it is also impossible to understand. This is a paradox but it is not necessarily a frivolous one. If a truly new language were invented it would initially be incomprehensible to everyone but its inventor. The paradox thus calls attention to certain aspects of the crisis of modern consciousness that are more evident in literature than in painting and sculpture. This, in one sense, is the meaning of the poetry of nothing—its way, to quote Alfred Barr once again, of helping us "see and understand" experience.

II

Am I not a soluble fish? Since I was born under the sign of Pisces and man is soluble in his own thought.

—André Breton

Since Francis Bacon's *Advancement of Learning* it has been recognized that there is a tension between science and natural language. Science attempts to be universal while natural language is local. Science also seeks to be arbitrary in the sense of depending on logic rather than on myth or religion or tradition. It will go wherever its logic takes it. Language, on the other hand, is not arbitrary. We inherit our language, we do not create it. As we learn it, it shapes our consciousness. We accept it passively—its phonetics, its grammar, its syntax, its idioms. It is natural, a given, and what is natural is the opposite of what is arbitrary.

Because each human mind is formed by a natural language, which, in turn, is a vehicle of the history of a specific culture, the achievement of true arbitrariness in thought and expression is extremely difficult. Although we live in an unconventional world, we are always being trapped into the conventional by the association of ideas forced on us by language. The way out of the trap is to destabilize normal linguistic processes by imposing nonlinguistic rules on them. The most effective rules will be entirely arbitrary—hence random. Randomness is therefore a recurrent theme in efforts to create a linguistic art comparable to abstract art. It is also an element—though a less crucial one—in efforts to break away from traditional modes of visual and auditory representation; to break away, for example, from imitative habits in painting and traditional melodies, scales, and rhythms in music.

To be transparent a natural language would have to be equally intelligible to all readers or listeners. No natural languages can begin to meet this condition. Natural languages become increasingly transparent as they are imposed on ever larger geographical areas by imperialism or a melting pot philosophy, but so far in history, imperialism has tended to create resentment that has eventually halted the spread of every natural language. This is evident in the history of Greek, Arabic, Chinese, Spanish, French, English, and Russian.

To spread easily a language should be neutral. It should not be associated with the tyranny of one society over another but should be equally convenient for all societies. Historically, the closest approximation of this limited kind of transparency in the Western world has been medieval-Latin. By the time Latin became the universal language of the establishment in medieval Europe it had ceased to be spoken by any of the peoples who used it. It was a dead language, hence an arbitrary choice. It achieved transparency within its limited geographic region largely because the culture that had produced it had disappeared. Belonging to nobody, it suddenly belonged to everybody. By the same token, it had ceased to be a natural language. It had to be taught, much as mathematics is taught today. When learned, it became the passport into an international managerial elite whose culture was different in kind from all the local cultures it administered.

The nineteenth century brought a wave of enthusiasm for what Tennyson, in *Locksley Hall,* called "the parliament of man, the Federation of the World." Since there was no possibility of reviving Latin in the Age of Telegraphy, efforts turned to the creation of a synthetic language. The most notable figure in this movement was Ludwig Zamenhof, a Polish physician who called his language Esperanto—the language of hope. The first requirement of a universal synthetic language is that it be easy to learn. Zamenhof interpreted this requirement in terms of Western European languages. The result was a language with a minimum of inflections, a romance syntax, and a vocabulary as rich as possible in romance, germanic, and slavic cognates. Esperanto was a notable effort but it was never successful. Today, Latin is still taught in a dwindling number of schools, but Esperanto is a memory.

Any use of the phonetics or vocabulary or grammar or literary conventions of a natural language makes a universal language opaque. Even if it had been fully successful, Esperanto would have been transparent only within the area of the Western European family of languages from which its grammar and vocabulary were drawn. In theory, pure nonsense words should be transparent because they are equally unintelligible to everyone, unless, by accident, a word that is nonsense in 4,999 of the world's languages happens to be the name for glaucoma in the 5,000th. But what looks good in theory turns out to be unworkable in practice. In creating nonsense words the mind follows the patterns of its natural language. A German or a Czech or a Japanese or an English nonsense word tends to sound German or Czech or Japanese or English because of its phonemes and syllabification. The alternative is to create a language of randomly chosen sounds. Even sounds, however, conspire to meaning because when uttered they tend to follow the patterns of elementary literary forms—lament, expression of joy, satisfaction, and the like—with the further qualification that these literary forms tend to be specific to individual language groups and may be quite unintelligible beyond them. On the other hand, if the sounds can be combined as well as selected by a random process, they will have no culturally determined form and hence should be perfectly transparent.

At least when uttered. When they are printed a whole new range of problems arises because some alphabets are phonetic and others are ideographic. Printing sounds in a Roman alphabet localizes them just as much as printing them in Chinese ideographs. The perfectly transparent printed poem would be in an alphabet as randomly created—and hence as unintelligible—as the sounds themselves.

This line of thought leads to a dead end. It reveals the fact that all natural languages are irrevocably tied to history and that the idea of escaping from this history is an illusion. The only way to escape completely is to compose unintelligible, randomly selected sounds in an alphabet that has never been used, which is equivalent to abandoning natural language for an entirely arbitrary language that no one can understand.

The history of efforts to create transparent language is therefore a history of compromise. It is intriguing and probably highly significant that the first self-conscious efforts to create nonsense occurred during the rise of industrialism and that the most successful English poet in this vein was a mathematician who wrote under a pseudonym and had a fondness for small girls. Significant or not, Lewis Carroll's solution to the problem of nonsense was to introduce nonsense words into otherwise conventional English sentences. This practice reduces even the limited transparency of the nonsense. The coined words become vehicles of grammatical meaning. That is, even though they have no lexical meaning, they become, in context, recognizable subjects, objects, verbs, adjectives and the like for the reader who is familiar with English. The point is illustrated by the following stanza from Carroll's poem "Jabberwocky":

> And, as in uffish thought he stood,
>   The Jabberwock, with eyes of flame,
> Came whiffling through the tulgy wood,
>   And burbled as it came!

Although we cannot say exactly what a Jabberwock is, we know it is a noun singular, subject of *came*. But we know more. Because the poem in which this stanza occurs is based on the conventional medieval literary form of the knightly quest, we conclude that the Jabberwock is a monster that has to be slain by the hero. We know, too, that the Jabberwock inhabits a tulgy wood. It has the characteristics of an animal, and its whiffles and burblings are both sinister and delightful. They reinforce the literary convention and the parody.

"Jabberwocky" is amusing, but the humor would be lost on a Japanese reader. A perfectly transparent language must be emptied of all associations with natural and local languages. Its poetry should be, we might say, a poetry of nothing, as devoid of meaning as the abstractions of a randomly instructed program on a computer.

Is this possible in language? In various ways the search for a transparent poetry has been carried on since the early twentieth century with full consciousness of the objective. As we have seen, Mallarmé sensed both the objective and the difficulty of achieving it. In "Un Coup de Dés" the need of the human mind for pattern is opposed to the meaninglessness of reality. The true meaninglessness of the world threatens to overwhelm the mind, but the mind stubbornly and heroically throws the dice again and imposes another randomly selected pattern on the emptiness of the world.

As previously noted, three movements in contemporary poetry illustrate the impulse to carry the ideal of transparency beyond Mallarmé: dada, concrete poetry, and algorithmic poetry. These movements are fascinating because they seem to fly in the face of the characteristics of natural languages. They are as instructive in their failures as in their successes, and their successes, though not immediately obvious, are by no means insignificant.

Dada is the most widely known of these movements. Although it achieves a high degree of transparency while still using words from natural languages, it appears incapable of making statements about the human condition that could be considered significant. "Appears" is the right word here because dada may be expressing something that we can still understand only imperfectly; namely, the isolation of the mind in technological society from the comforts and sacred values of history. If so, dada expresses the movement of humanity out of Nature and toward the habitat of scientific universals. Another possibility, which seems more in accord with the nature of natural languages, is that dada is doomed to failure from the start. To ask a natural language to embody the experience of a technological society may be like asking earth to symbolize fire.

The key to dada is randomness. Achieving randomness, however, is more difficult than it sounds. In certain areas of high technology, randomness is essential. Consequently the subject has been explored in depth. All simple approaches to randomness produce patterns. A typical method of constructing a dada poem, for example, is cutting up phrases or words from a newspaper, stirring them in a hat, and pasting them on a piece of paper in the order in which they are withdrawn. Obviously, the words come from a natural language, and it is equally obvious that, being printed, they are in a visual medium (the Roman alphabet) that is opaque rather than transparent. Even if we ignore these objections, we still confront the fact that the words are an inadequate statistical sample of the words in the natural language from which they were drawn. They are not arbitrary. They reflect the personal idiosyncrasies of the audience to which they were directed, the state of the language at the time when the article was written, and the like. These are all determined by history. An article on the culture of grapes from a French newspaper published in 1880, for example, will use a vocabulary different from an article on the same subject published in 1970. Words clipped from an issue of *Time Magazine* will have a different bias from words clipped from an article in *The Rolling Stone* of the same year. Unfortunately, alternate strategies for achieving randomness have other defects. Decisions about word choice might be made by flipping a coin or throwing dice in the manner of Mallarmé's poem. But coins and dice are biased and become more so as they are used because of wear. It therefore seems that perfect randomness is an ideal that can be approached but never attained. These facts are remote from everyday experience and probably irrelevant to dada, but they form a wall around all efforts to achieve transparency in language and are therefore worth noting.

Dada originated in Zurich in 1916. According to the most common account, the word was found by inserting a paper-knife in the pages of an uncut Larousse dictionary of French and German. When the page was opened the point of the knife was found to be resting on the mysterious and pregnant word *dada*. Literary historians have interpreted the word in a variety of ways: sociological, political, psychological, and the like. In his history *Dada* (1961) Willy Verkauf, for example, claims that it was a movement to protest the "senseless mass murder" of the First World War, and "the hectic outcry of the tormented creature in the artist, of his prophetic, admonishing, tormented conscience." This is impressive rhetoric, but it seems completely out of key with the accounts which Tristian Tzara, the founder of the movement, gives of the playful atmosphere in which dada was born. The same point may be made of Hans Knutter's suggestion that dada was a form of infantile regression from the horrors of the adult world, and the commonplace assertion that dada was motivated by a perverse desire by artists to upset the complacent middle class (*épater le bourgeoisie*).

Tristian Tzara claims that the basic attraction of the word was that it had no meaning. It meant nothing, and nothing is the true subject of dada. In his *Dada Manifesto* of 1918 Tzara attacked the ideologues who were trying to impose conventional literary values on the movement: "[It is] a word that means nothing. . . . [But] the first thought that occurs to these people is bacteriological in origin: to find its etymological or at least its historical or psychological origin. We see by the papers that the Kru Negroes call the tail of a holy cow Dada. The cube and the mother in a certain district of Italy are called Dada. A hobby horse and a nurse both in Russian and Rumanian: Dada. Some learned journalists regard it as an art for babies." All these efforts to attach dada to history contradict its basic intention.

Nothing is not used by Tzara to mean nihilism—a bitter and frequently despairing rejection of traditional values—but to affirm the liberating power of the arbitrary. In becoming "nothing" poetry escapes the trap of history—of ideology, of flaccid poetic diction, of tired canons of beauty, and the like—and can become anything. A perfectly transparent poem can become everything simply because it is not tied to one specific meaning. A Rorschach ink-blot is not nihilistic in the normal sense of that term; like dada it is simply nothing. Its lack of meaning is its value. The viewer fills it with the content of his or her own subconscious, just as the Eiffel Tower manages to be all things to all men by virtue of its freedom from historically defined architectural forms.

Shortly after being discovered, dada moved to Paris where it attracted the interest of poets and artists like Marcel Duchamp, Man Ray, André Breton, Paul Eluard, Louis Aragon, Erik Satie, Jean Arp, Francis Picabia, and others. Significant relations developed between the dadists and the futurist and cubist painters who were seeking new forms of visual expression. Verkauf sees the Paris period as decadent and claims, against all evidence, that dada was opposed to abstract art. This appears, like much else in Verkauf, to be the reflection of a political bias in favor of art that makes strong social statements. At any rate, the dada coalition was always a loose one. In the 1920s it dissolved. Some of the dadists followed Aragon into the Communist party and others followed Breton into French surrealism.

Eugene Jolas claims to have invented one of the purest and most translucent forms of dada, the sound poem. He explains it as follows:

> I invented a new species of verse, "verse without words," or sound poems.... I had a special costume designed for it. My legs were covered with a cothurnus of luminous blue cardboard, which reached up to my hips so that I looked like an obelisk.... I recited the following:
>
> gadja beri bimba
> glandridi lauli lomni cadori
> gadjaimo bim beri glassala
> glandridi glassala tuffm i zunbrabism.
>
> ... We should withdraw into the innermost alchemy of the word, and even surrender the word, in this way conserving for poetry its sacred domain.

Rudolf Klein attributes this poem and the comment on it to Hugo Ball, proprietor of the Cabaret Voltaire in Zurich where dada began. Whether the author was Jolas or Ball, the poem clearly illustrates the limits of transparency even when all natural words have been abandoned. Its phonetic values and regularities suggest a Western European imitation of an unknown African language. In spite of this defect, however, it represents a completely logical solution to the problem of linguistic transparency.

The master of the sound poem was Kurt Schwitters, who once composed a whole sound sonata in four movements. A more concise example of his art is *W*, a poem of one letter. Moholy-Nagy, who achieved international fame as a member of the Bauhaus, describes Schwitters's recitation of the poem as follows:

> He showed the audience a poem containing only one letter on a sheet: *W*. Then he started to "recite" it with slowly rising voice. The consonant varied from a whisper to the sound of a wailing siren till at the end he barked with a shockingly loud tone.

Moholy-Nagy regards this recitation as a lament for the horrors of the First World War. Kurt Schwitters, however, was apparently nonpolitical and more interested in language than in trench warfare. At the same time, it is worth noting that pure abstraction often has deep religious or instinctual connotation. Moholy-Nagy uses primitive words to describe Schwitters's recitation: *whisper, wail, barked.* Jolas (or Ball) remarked that during the recitation of the sound poem "gadji beri bimba," "I . . . noticed that my voice, which seemed to have no other choice, had assumed the age-old cadence of sacerdotal lamentation, like the chanting of the Mass." The poem, in other words, is very close to a common and ancient religious phenomenon, glossolalia, or speaking in tongues. The *W* poem of Kurt Schwitters moves in a similar manner toward an approximation of what might be called today the primal scream. This is analogous to the tendency of simple geometric objects—a tower, a sphere, a circle—to be interpreted by viewers in sexual terms. The point, however, is incidental. The basic object of sound poetry is correctly identified by Maholy-Nagy in a later comment on Schwitters:

> The only possible solution [to the stifling of poetry by convention] seemed to be a return to the elements of poetry, to noise and articulated sound, which are fundamental to all languages. Schwitters realized the prophecy of Rimbaud, inventing words "accessible to all five senses." His poem *Ursonata* is a poem thirty-five minutes in duration. . . . The words used do not exist in any language; they have no logical, only an emotional context.

A notorious dada technique for achieving transparency in language was clipping words from journals. While this technique retains the words of a natural language and the words, themselves, are not a true cross-section even of that language, the result is expression with a high degree of randomness. Tzara gives the formula for this kind of poetry and a sample poem:

> To make a dadist poem
> Take a newspaper.
> Take a pair of scissors.
> Choose an article as long as you are planning to make your poem.
> Cut out the article.
> Then cut out each of the words that make up the article and put them in a bag.
> Shake it gently.

Then take out the scraps one after the other in the order in which they left the bag.
Copy conscientiously.
The poem will be like you.
And here you are a writer, infinitely original, endowed with a sensibility that is charming, though beyond the understanding of the vulgar.

Example:

When the dogs cross the air in a diamond like the
ideas and the appendix of the meanings show the hour
of the awakening program (The title is my own.)

price they are yesterday agreeing afterwards paintings
Appreciate the dream epoch of the eyes pompously
than recite the gospel made darkness group the
apotheosis imagine he said fatality power of flowers. . . .

The effect is defined by Richard Huelsenbeck in his *Collective Dada Manifesto* of 1920. The random poem "makes words into individuals; out of the letters spelling words, steps the woods with its treetops." Words, however, are less transparent than sounds. In spite of the lack of grammar and syntax, Tzara's words trap the reader in their natural meanings. The literary critic buried in every psyche longs to damn them as bare-faced fraud or trace their subtle meanings.

In *Science and the Modern World* Alfred North Whitehead observes that it takes an extraordinary intelligence to contemplate the obvious. One of the prime tasks of the poetry—it may be *the* prime task—is to contemplate the obvious. In the famous definition of poetry that Coleridge offers in Chapter xiv of his *Biographia Literaria,* the basic appeal of poetry is said to be its capacity for "awakening the mind's attention from the lethargy of custom and directing it to the loveliness and the wonders of the world about us; an inexhaustible treasure, but for which, in consequence of the film of familiar and selfish solicitude, we have eyes, yet see not, ears that hear not, and hearts that neither feel nor understand."

Whether or not the poets of dada were revealing unappreciated beauties and wonders, their fascination with typography and newspapers suggests that they were contemplating the obvious transformation to which language was being subjected during the early twentieth century by the mass media. Marcel Duchamp had presented commonplace commercially produced objects—bicycle wheels and urinals, for example—as though they were works of art, and the practice is now widely followed by museums that exhibit motorcars, typewriters, and sewing machines with all the reverence that used to be reserved for Michelangelo and Vermeer.

Is it not a literary manifestation of the same impulse to make poems out of headlines clipped from newspapers in the manner of André Breton (fig. 2)? To test this theory one need only try to imagine how today's newspaper would appear to a reader unfamiliar with the conventions of modern journalism. It would appear to be a surrealistic poem—a haphazard mosaic of columns of different lengths, of photographs, of headlines of different sizes, and of advertisements. The untrained reader would find himself following a story about political corruption, then breaking off in mid-sentence to begin a report on SALT negotiations, breaking off again to read about a teen-ager who died in a fire, then breaking off to read about Mexican wetbacks, then breaking off again ... and so forth. The only element connecting the stories on the front page is an accident: they all occurred within twenty-four hours before the paper was published. The headlines become pure dada once the events they identify are forgotten. Here is a sample from a 1978 issue of the *Washington Post*:

Fig. 2. Poem made by André Breton by clipping words from a newspaper

MANIFESTE

POÈME

Un éclat de rire
de saphir dans l'île de Ceylan

Les plus belles pailles
ONT LE TEINT FANÉ
SOUS LES VERROUS

dans une ferme isolée
AU JOUR LE JOUR
s'aggrave
l'agréable

Une voie carrossable
vous conduit au bord de l'inconnu

le café
prêche pour son saint
L'ARTISAN QUOTIDIEN DE VOTRE BEAUTÉ
Madame,

Suburbs Push Spartan Water Habits
Thurmond's Switch
Old Celebrations, New Translations, Gossip, and Ghosts
Nambi's Dunes Hide Wealth of Diamonds
Energy in August
Orioles Toppled by Rare Blasts from Nordhagen
Sounders Earn Date With Cosmos
Weaver Gives Thumb Again

In a sense, Tzara and his friends were not inventing anything new; they were merely imitating what had already arrived.

By 1939 dada had expired, a victim of the general sense that life was real and life was earnest and about to get a lot more so. A new movement which traced some of its most typical interests to dada appeared, however, in the early 1950s. It originated more or less simultaneously in Brazil and Switzerland and centered around what is called concrete poetry. After the Brazilian and Swiss writers learned of each other's work, they became aware of similar experiments elsewhere. Evidently, concrete poetry was not an isolated phenomenon but a general trend toward a new kind of world literature reflecting a new, international consciousness. The Brazilians traced its ancestry to Mallarmé, Ezra Pound, and e. e. cummings, and the Swiss to Tristian Tzara, Jean Arp, and Kurt Schwitters. The Italians stressed the contribution of futurism, and Marinetti, the chief spokesman for futurism, survived to offer advice and counsel to the Italian concrete poets of the 1950s.

Concrete poetry does not share the interest of dada in nothing and is generally indifferent to the sensational "happenings" that Tzara and Duchamp so much enjoyed. However, many concrete poets accept the thesis that language in the traditional sense is dead. It has become so corrupted by political slogans, mass advertising, and stale literary conventions that it has ceased to be expressive. It is like a glass of water in which all the colors of the watercolor box have been mixed. The water is not rainbow colored but mud colored. As Piet Mondrian, Theo van Doesburg, and Anthony Koh announced in a manifesto composed in the 1920s:

> The Word is impotent
> asthmatic and sentimental poetry
> the "me" and the "it". . . .
> the dregs of an exhausted era.

The alternative to the asthmatic impotence of words is a language as pure as mathematics. In an important essay on the new poetics, the Czech critic Zdnek Baborka argues that there are two human natures. The first is the "natural" human nature reflected in history. The second is the rational human nature expressed in science. Natural human nature is corrupt and debased. We know this from the sad, bloody record of history and from the Christian doctrine of original sin. The way out of the quagmire of corrupt human nature is "the unnatural road, which has given [man] the human qualities that have enabled him to create the greatest works of civilization, and which is able to replace human nature entirely." Instead of opposing science as "dehumanizing," artists should adopt not only its subjects but its detachment, its rationalism, and its universality.

This point of view is frequently echoed in concrete poetic theory. When Carlo Belloni published his initial experiments entitled *Testi-Murali (Wall-texts)*, Marinetti wrote in the introduction, "these text poems anticipate a language of word-signs set in the communications network of a mathematical civilization." Poems, Belloni argued, should be "anonymous, silent, almost invisible: words set free in an almost transparent medium." The epigraph of Eugen Gomringer's journal *Konkrete Poesie/Poesia concreta* was: "Concrete poetry is the aesthetic chapter of the universal linguistic form of our epoch." Gomringer argued that concrete poetry expresses "the contemporary scientific-technical view of the world. . . . I am therefore convinced that concrete poetry is the process of realizing the idea of a universal poetry." Mary Ellen Solt, the most knowledgeable authority on the subject writing in English, seems to agree. The title of her book is *Concrete Poetry: A World View*.

The desire to create a form of expression as pure as science explains those concrete poems that seek to become pure visual experience, emptied of lexical meaning. Mary Ellen Solt's "Moonshot Sonnet" (fig. 3) is an example. Alternatively, a poem can aspire to the condition of music by becoming pure sound in the manner of Mathias Goeritz's "The Echo of the Gold," in which sound becomes visual (fig. 4), or Ladislav Novák's "Magic of a Summer Night," in which the text, while retaining a strong visual element, is really a musical score for voice (fig. 5).

Much concrete poetry fails to meet these standards. It succumbs to the ancient and corrupt allure of language. Instead of reaching for transparency it affirms the natural meanings of words and uses visual devices to emphasize them. Evidently, it is trying to rehabilitate language rather than transcend it. Such poems have a pronounced lyric quality. The difference between them and traditional romantic lyrics is that they are minimal—attention is focused on a few words or a single word. "Loneliness" by e. e. cummings uses four words:

```
l(a

le
af
fa

ll

s)
one
l

iness
```

Here the lexical meaning of loneliness is reinforced by the image of a falling leaf. The image is both rhetorical and visual: the poem "falls" as one reads it. *One* and *liness* in the seventh, eighth, and ninth lines further emphasize the theme. Aside from its brevity and typography the poem is entirely conventional. The objective is not to decenter language but to restore it. A similar impulse is evident in a somewhat more elaborate piece by Richard Kostelanetz (fig. 6). Here language is not being used to achieve transparency but to give English some of the qualities of Chinese ideographs.

Fig. 3. Mary Ellen Solt: "Moonshot Sonnet"

Fig. 4. Mathias Goeritz: "The Echo of the Gold"

Fig. 5. Ladislav Novák: "Magic of a Summer Night"

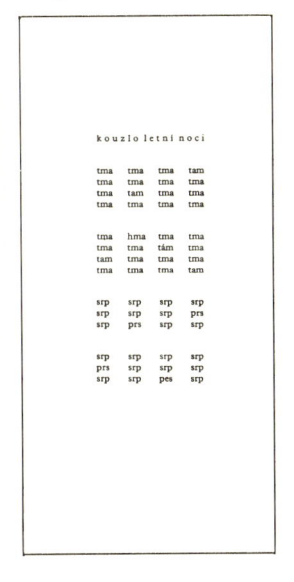

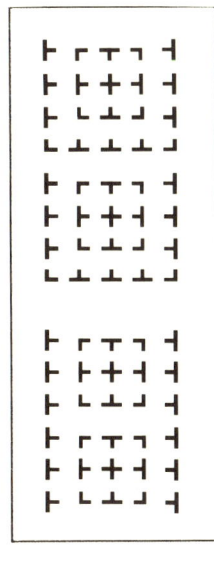

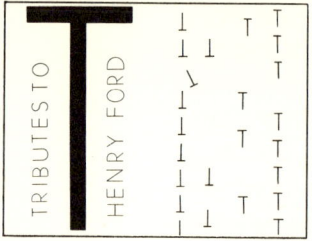

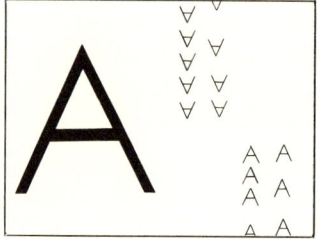

Fig. 6. Richard Kostelanetz: "Tributes to Henry Ford"

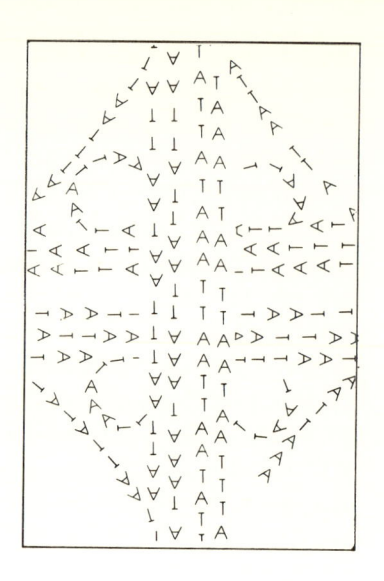

When Eugen Gomringer began to write concrete poems, he turned from German, which he had been using for conventional sonnets, to Spanish. Since he was born in Bolivia, to revert to Spanish was to establish a link with his past. Concrete poetry, he explained, "must be closely bound up with the challenge of individual existence: with the individual's 'Life with Language'." Pierre Garnier argued in his *Manifesto* of 1962 that concrete poetry will make the word "holy again," while Ian Finley, a Scots poet, announced that it "offers a tangible image of goodness and sanity." These are commendable sentiments. They are opposite to the theory of Zdnek Baborka that poetry should transcend natural humanity, not to mention the announcement by the Japanese concrete poet, Kitasono Katue, that the insights of Zen have "driven [words] away as worthless rubbish."

The lyric impulse is predominant in a great many poems that are labeled "concrete." Eugen Gomringer's "Avenidas" is a hymn to beautiful and traditional ideas (fig. 7). Its lyricism is so strong that a traditionalist might complain that it verges on the sentimental. "Silencio" is clearly an artistic advance because the superfluous sentiment has been pruned away, while the typographical arrangement expresses and reinforces the meaning in the way that Chinese calligraphy reinforces the meaning of a

Chinese poem (fig. 8). Decio Pignatari's "Beba" is not only derived from a found concrete poem—the Coca-Cola bottle—it is also a waspish satire on the spread of Madison Avenue hucksterism in South America (fig. 9). "Schützengraben" (the word means *trench*) by Ernst Jandl is more of a sound than a sight poem (fig. 10) and uses the technique of exploded orthography found in e. e. cummings's "Loneliness." It sputters with machine guns and whines with shell fire. The result is a powerful statement of the real meaning of the word. Edwin Morgan's "Computer Christmas Card" is more mathematical—it is based on random combinations and recombinations of a few words—but equally expressive (fig. 11). A final example by Oswald Wiener offers a sophisticated epistemological statement about the relation between I (*Ich*) and thou (*Du*) in minimal terms (fig. 12).

In theory, concrete poetry seeks the transparency of science. In practice the words that are its raw material draw it back toward traditional modes of poetry. Horace observed that if you push Nature out of the front door she comes in again at the back. In the case of concrete poetry, an impulse that begins by assuming the death of the word ends by using the energies of art to assert, perhaps nostalgically, the life that words retain.

Fig. 7. Eugen Gomringer: "Avenidas"

Fig. 8. Eugen Gomringer: "Silencio"

Fig. 9. Décio Pignatari: "Beba"

```
avenidas
avenidas y flores


flores
flores y mujeres


avenidas
avenidas y mujeres


avenidas y flores y mujeres y
un admirador
```

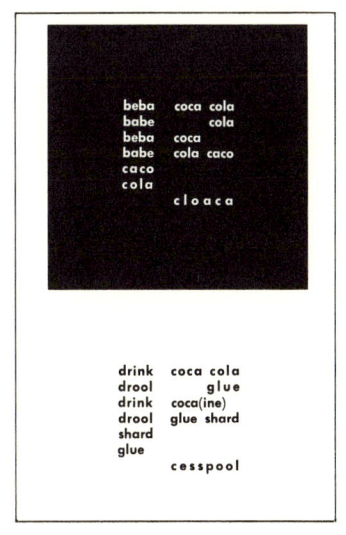

```
silencio silencio silencio
silencio silencio silencio
silencio          silencio
silencio silencio silencio
silencio silencio silencio
```

```
beba    coca cola
babe         cola
beba    coca
babe    cola caco
caco
cola
        cloaca




drink   coca cola
drool        glue
drink   coca(ine)
drool   glue shard
shard
glue
        cesspool
```

A curious example of an art that is half-way between language and science is provided by algorithmic poetry. The tradition of mathematical art is as old as the Golden Section and the musical proportions of Pythagoras. Renaissance musicians experimented with a broad array of arbitrary systems of composition based on number, including compositions based on dice throws. In the twentieth century Joseph Schillinger created "a scientific system of musical composition" based on what he considered, rightly or wrongly, mathematical transformations of such visual images as the skyline of New York and the contours of the Andes. Mathematical elements are also common in literature. The Greeks and Romans thought of meter as "number." During the Renaissance metrical numbers were supplemented by numerological symbolism expressed in stanzaic forms, arrangements of rhyme and half-rhyme, and the like. Edmund Spenser's *Epithalamion,* for example, is an elaborate numerical composition based on astronomical and calendrical facts. These facts are explained by A. Kent Hieatt in *Short Time's Endless Moment.* The *Epithalamion* balances the solar against the lunar year, and balances day against night in a way that defines the latitude where Spenser's marriage took place and the time of the year when the service was performed. A similar use of calendrical lore is apparent in Spenser's *Amoretti,* in which each

Fig. 10. Ernst Jandl:
"Schützengraben"

```
schtzngrmm
schtzngrmm
t-t-t-t
t-t-t-t
grrrmmmmm
t-t-t-t
s———c———h
tzngrmm
tzngrmm
tzngrmm
grrrmmmmm
schtzn
schtzn
t-t-t-t
t-t-t-t
schtzngrmm
schtzngrmm
tssssssssssssssssss
grrt
grrrrrt
grrrrrrrrt
scht
scht
t-t-t-t-t-t-t-t-t
scht
tzngrmm
tzngrmm
t-t-t-t-t-t-t-t-t
scht
scht
scht
scht
grrrrrrrrrrrrrrrrrrrrrrr
t-tt
```

Fig. 11. Edwin Morgan:
"The Computer's First
Christmas Card"

```
        jollymerry
        hollyberry
        jollyberry
        merryholly
        happyjolly
        jollyjelly
        jellybelly
        bellymerry
        hollyheppy
        jollyMolly
        marryJerry
        merryHarry
        hoppyBarry
        heppyJarry
        boppyheppy
        berryjorry
        jorryjolly
        moppyjelly
        Mollymerry
        Jerryjolly
        bellyboppy
        jorryhoppy
        hollymoppy
        Barrymerry
        Jarryhappy
        happyboppy
        boppyjolly
        jollymerry
        merrymerry
        merrymerry
        merryChris
        ammerryasa
        Chrismerry
        ASMERRYCHR
        YSANTHEMUM
```

Fig. 12. Oswald Wiener:
"du/dich/ich"

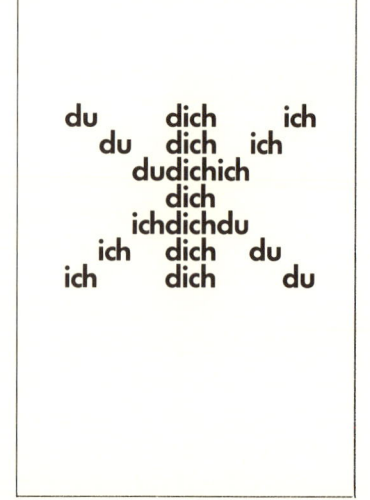

```
  du      dich      ich
   du     dich    ich
        dudichich
           dich
         ichdichdu
     ich   dich   du
  ich     dich      du
```

sonnet of the central group is identified with a day during the Lenten season of 1594.

In these examples numerological influence creates a level of organization halfway between the organization of individual lines provided by meter and the organization of whole poems provided by genre conventions. Alastair Fowler, an authority on numerological poetry, writes, "In poetry numerological structure often forms a level of organization intermediate in scale and externality between metrical patterns on the one hand and structure as ordinarily understood on the other. . . . It is probably no exaggeration to say that most good literary works—indeed, most craftsmanlike works—were organized at this stratum until the eighteenth century at least." Abraham Cowley believed that numerology was divinely ordained. In a note to *Davideis* (1656) he wrote, "The Scripture witnesses that the World was made in *Number, Weight,* and *Measure,* which are all qualities of a good Poem. This order and proportion of things is the true Musick of the World."

One way to achieve "true musick" in poetry is to include mathematical elements in its composition. Since mathematics is one thing and natural language another, mathematical patterns always distort natural language. The artist has two options. He can attempt to conceal them and appear "natural," or he can use the unnatural effects they create as positive and expressive devices. Meter is a good example. No one speaks English naturally in iambic pentameter. In drama the use of blank verse dialogue conflicts with the impulse toward realism. Shakespeare's early plays use a strong iambic pentameter line in which the artificiality is often emphasized by rhyme. In the great tragedies, however, the blank verse is de-emphasized by metrical irregularities, enjambment, and similar devices. When spoken by a trained actor, its metrical structure is almost completely concealed. Eventually, of course, English drama abandoned meter entirely and it is now written in prose. The basic idea of epic, on the other hand, is that it should be larger than life. The last thing the writer of an epic wants is a passage that sounds like ordinary conversation. Consequently, in *Paradise Lost* Milton emphasizes the meter. The artificiality that this strategy produces becomes a means of expressing the difference between the epic characters and the man on the street.

Some twentieth-century poetry is explicitly mathematical and is carried on in the spirit of a game. The object of the game is to see how far arbitrary rules—algorithms—can be applied to language before intelligibility is completely lost; or, in other words, how far language can be pushed without disappearing. The play element is significant because it is the literary equivalent of the spirit of play evident in the work of modern artists like Duchamp, Miró, and Calder, and is echoed in "serious" literature like Joyce's *Finnegans Wake* (from which the word *quark* was taken by the physicist Murray Gell-Mann) and the poems of e. e. cummings and Wallace Stevens.

Like concrete poetry, algorithmic poetry is an international movement. It is produced by French, Belgian, Italian, and American poets. Some of them have formed a loosely organized group called Oulipo, which is an acronym for *Ouvroir de Litterature Potentielle*—Workshop of Potential Literature. A book on this group was published by Gallimard in 1973 titled *La Litterature Potentielle* (*Creations, Re-Creations, Recreations*).

Oulipo has produced what must be one of the most ambitious creations in the history of poetry. It is Raymond Gueneau's *Cent Mille Millarde de Poems—A Hundred Thousand Billion Poems.* This book, also published by Gallimard, consists of ten sonnets. Each is printed on the right-hand side of a page, and each page is cut into 14 strips, one line to a strip. By turning the strips in random fashion the reader creates his own sonnet. In fact, it is impossible to turn the strips in a way that does not produce a sonnet. The number of sonnets possible is 10^{14} or one hundred thousand billion, "all structurally perfect and making sense." Mathematics has here transcended the microdot. A literary collection that would strain the stack resources of the New York Public Library has been packed into a single small volume.

Different algorithms produce different literary genres. One common genre is the lipogram, which is a composition that omits one or more letters of the alphabet. This genre was known in the Middle Ages and it has been revived. Ernest Wright's *Gadsby* (1939) and Georges Perec's *La Disparition* (1969) are novels that never use the letter *e*. A more complex algorithm produces the isogram. Martin Gardner, to whose discussion of Oulipo this section is heavily indebted, observes that the eleven most common letters in French spell the word *ulceration*. A composition can be created that is limited to these letters alone or permits the use of additional letters at predetermined intervals. In English the twelve most frequent letters, in order of decreasing frequency, are *etaoin shrdlu*. (Shrdlu, incidentally, is the name of a computer program for artificial intelligence.) These words formed the first and second columns respectively on the keyboards of old-style linotype machines. When embossed on a linotype slug they become a concrete poem of nearly perfect transparency. Another alphabetical algorithm creates the snowballing poem in which each word is one letter longer than the one before it. Jean Dunnington has created a compound genre: the snowballing iceogram. Here, for example, is a dirge for a Scottie drowned at a picnic which includes an ironic digression on the indifference of Nature to human sorrow:

> O,
> on!
> One
> done.
> Drone
> Droned.
> Drowned.

Yet another variation of the alphabetical algorithm is the following apostrophe of a crow to a scarecrow written by A. Ross Ekler of the Bell Telephone Laboratories:

> Hey, be seedy! He effigy, hate-shy jaky
> yellow man, o peek, you are rusty, you've
> edible, you ex-wise he!

The poems of Dunnington and Ekler are examples of the kind of traditionalism that can also be observed in the lyric tendency of certain concrete poets. It is a nostalgic loyalty to natural language and meaning in spite of the pull of mathematics and pure sound. Traditionalism is also evident in the following example by Demitri Borgmann of a snowballing composition of twenty words:

> I do not know why family doctors acquired
> illegibly perplexing handwriting; nevertheless,
> extraordinary pharmaceutical intellectuality,
> counterbalancing indecipherability, transcendentalizes
> intercommunications' incomprehensibleness.

Note that the sentence begins in prose but veers toward poetry as the rigors of the algorithm begin to be felt. In spite of the sense of increasing complexity, the sentence retains a conventional meaning.

Möbius poetry is poetry formed by writing two different poems on a Möbius strip and reading it continuously. An alternating sequence of lines occurs that creates a new composition. Another Oulipo algorithm is called N + 7. It requires substituting for each noun in a passage the noun that appears at least seven nouns ahead in a standard dictionary. With *Webster's Collegiate Dictionary* (1953) as the standard source, Hamlet's "What a piece of work is man" becomes "What a piecer of workaday is manager." The new line is not *Hamlet*, but it has a poetic felicity of its own. The algorithm N + 14 produces: "What a Pierian of working capital is manchet." (*Manchet* means a loaf of bread.) That even this transformation is not entirely without meaning illustrates the stubborn desire of the mind to discover meaning in almost any statement. There is an element in all poetry of surprise and originality. Algorithms distort language in surprising and unpredictable ways and therefore produce effects that are likely to seem poetic. Are they poetic? Distinguishing between seeming and being is not always as easy as it looks. Ridicule and outrage consistently greet new works of art that are later accepted as masterpieces—consider James Joyce and Pablo Picasso. Perhaps a few algorithmic poems that seem trivial today will eventually be considered classics. Most algorithmic poetry, however, is play. It has no pretensions. But it cannot be dismissed. Martin Gardner observes, "Ingenious, I hear you say, but how frivolous, and what a sad waste of creative energy. Yet does it not bring home to us how a culture's language, with its mysterious blend of sound and meaning, is a structure with an independent life of its own?"

The search for the "independent life" of language is characteristic of the twentieth century. It stems from despair over the degree to which the use of language is conditioned by history, so that words become vehicles for conventions rather than current experience. But language can assert its independent life only by abandoning the lexical meanings and grammatical forms that it inherits from history. Dada, concrete poetry, and algorithmic poetry can be understood as attempts to liberate language and by doing this to liberate man so that he can confront his present situation. These attempts are interesting but they always collide with the fact that language *is* a vehicle for meaning and that meaning is always determined by history. They collide, in other words, with the irreducible conservatism of language. When this happens, they must opt for the transparency of nothing, for the condition of pure abstraction, or admit defeat and surrender to the past, even though the past is an anachronism. Clearly the experiments are significant. Algorithms are as much a product of the human spirit as the *Mona Lisa,* perhaps more so in an absolute sense because they depend on conscious mental operations rather than forms supplied by Nature. The humanity that produces them has only begun to be explored. Before the twentieth century there was no road into the territory. Since we are now inhabitants of that territory, we are beginning to get an idea of its topography.

III

Painting and sculpture have accommodated themselves so successfully to twentieth-century experience that abstraction and its subcategories have been generally accepted as viable and meaningful languages. If they are not the standard languages of the art of the 1980s, they are among the standard languages. One seldom hears complaints that they are meaningless or fraudulent. One hears, instead, the quiet scramble of art investors at the auctions where the paintings are bought and sold.

Modern dance and music are less well acclimatized to the twentieth century than art. In spite of their basically abstract quality and the alliance, beginning with Pythagoras, between music and mathematics, they are still dominated by nostalgia. Verbal art, as has been noted, has been timid in comparison to painting. Many allegedly experimental poems and novels are attempts to dress traditional styles in modern clothing, while the truly experimental works still tend to be greeted with suspicion, if not outrage.

If we begin with the ancient idea of art as imitation, it is clear that modern painting and sculpture are imitating several kinds of experience. In one of its phases, cubism imitates the multifaceted view of reality that is created by the existence of many different but equally valid specialized studies, each with its own way of analyzing experience. As cubism grows more abstract, the traces of Nature that can be found in its early painting become more and more faint. They are being absorbed into a reality consisting of pure intellectual forms which are, essentially, the forms of analysis and perception. Abstract art also imitates the new reality being created by technology. Sculptors like Arp and Brancusi practice a kind of imitation that might be labeled "making the obvious obvious." Technology, that is, has surrounded modern man with brilliantly conceived technological objects. Yet, because we regard these objects as utilitarian, we ignore their aesthetic—that is, their immediately human—aspect. Airplane propellers and turbine blades are examples of mathematically precise surfaces that are very useful in attaining certain goals like flying or generating electricity. In addition to being useful, propellers and turbine blades have remarkable aesthetic properties. They speak to us even though we may not be conscious of what they are saying. Brancusi's highly finished steel and chromium sculptures abstract the aesthetic of mathematically precise surfaces from the uses that they commonly serve. The aesthetic properties then demand conscious recognition. They are all that is there. The viewer is forced to see them, and, to quote Alfred Barr once again, they help us "see and understand" the world we live in.

Are there not several ways in which efforts to create transparent poems are also imitations that help us "see and understand" experience?

First of all, they imitate a cultural reality suggested earlier by the quotation from Benjamin Lee Whorf: the modern world is fundamentally different from the traditionally-oriented world of the past. Physics has replaced mechanistic views of Nature with relativity and quantum theory. Although less advanced than physics, psychology, sociology, anthropology, economics, political science, and now biology promise to replace traditional views of social and personal activity with concepts based on empirical data rather than mythology and—in the case of biology—to replace the conservatism of the genetic code with the programs of the genetic engineers. The most obvious thing that the poetry of nothing imitates is, therefore, the inability of natural language, as a creation of thousands of years of history, to cope with this situation. The only thing more expressive of this situation than the poetry of nothing would be the poetry of silence, a fact which Mallarmé recognized and struggled against, because a poetry of silence is, ultimately, a poetry of surrender, of death.

A second object of imitation of the poetry of nothing is the new language that is emerging, more or less spontaneously and in response to demand, from technological society itself. The fact that Tristian Tzara and André Breton created poems by clipping words from newspapers has already been noted. The random quality of the front page of a newspaper is not accidental but essential. When, that is, we buy a copy of *War and*

Peace we buy it because we know more or less what it is and have decided we want it. When we buy a newspaper, part of our interest may be in a particular story, but part of the charm of the newspaper is that it will introduce us to the unexpected. The root of *news* is the word *new*. We know the newspaper will have a story on the latest plan for balancing the budget; but who can predict stories on a child falling into a well in Oklahoma, the production of human interferon from bacteria, a hurricane in Florida, the resignation of the superintendent of highways in North Dakota, a rebellion in Chad, and the like? Like the aesthetic of the airplane propeller, the aesthetic of the newspaper is invisible until divorced from its utilitarian matrix.

The dada quality found in newspapers is also evident in the art forms created by high technology. Movies are produced in "takes" that ignore the cause-effect patterns of their plots, and they are often seen by viewers from middle to end to beginning, with short subjects, cartoons, and previews coming between end and beginning, rather than in the familiar Aristotelian sequence of stage drama, from beginning to middle to end. This sort of discontinuity is minor, however, compared to the standard practice of American television which routinely cuts from the heroine watching her lover dying in the cancer ward to a commercial for toilet paper to a plug for underarm deodorants to a station break to a preview of the evening news and back to the heroine in the cancer ward. Even the happenings of dada look tame today when contrasted with such popular phenomena as demolition derbies, punk dress styles, singles bars, concerts by Led Zeppelin and KISS, Atari emporia, and supply-side economics.

Beyond such secondary phenomena, society has begun to make practical use of the strategies invented by dada and concrete poetry. Acronyms are nonhistorical and in that sense linguistically arbitrary formations. They are apparently essential in all advanced societies. They arise from the geometric increase of complex terminology in advanced societies and also from the tendency of this terminology to be temporary, a fact especially obvious in the case of managerial groups such as government agencies and their subdivisions. They are so useful that problems arise in disciplines that resist them. Medicine and biology, for example, have insisted since the Renaissance on creating their terminologies out of compounds of Greek and Latin roots. The result has been an increasingly impenetrable jargon that is difficult for physicians and biologists, let alone patients and laymen. Chemistry, conversely, began to create a fully acronymic language in the seventeenth century, and this language has now become a global, hence universal, language in spite of its Western origins.

If the languages of advanced societies are becoming hybrids of acronyms and natural words, the advertising industry of these societies has made extensive and powerful use of the strategies of concrete poetry. The Coca-Cola bottle, the Exxon sign, and the Delta Airlines logo use devices that, when they appear in concrete poetry, are frequently ridiculed. The reason for the practice is obvious. The identity of a product or a company is expressed in a compact, highly expressive language which is accessible to the speakers of many different natural languages, not to mention the illiterate members of the English-speaking world. It is, in other words, a transparent language, and in a global economy it has enormous commercial value.

The more esoteric uses of transparent languages are illustrated by the notation systems of mathematics and symbolic logic. Mathematics is now written in a notation that is standard worldwide. It uses an alphabet that is part Roman, part Greek, and part invented (e.g., the sign for infinity). The alphabet is complemented by operational symbols like plus, minus, multiply, and divide, and by quantitative symbols like equals and greater (or less) than. Computer programs look like purest dada to the uninitiated. The following brief instance may be considered a formal poem. Its aesthetic characteristics are brought to the surface by assigning it a title ("Meditations of a Robot") and printing it without explanation of its useful function. It is, in fact, a program for the defining functions of LISP, a language of artificial intelligence:

Meditations of a Robot

```
PUTPROP(QUOTE DEF)
   (QUOTE(LAMBDA(S A)
         (PUTPROP(CAR S)
            (CONS LAMBDA(CDR S))
            EXPR)))
   FEXPR)
PUTPROP(QUOTE DFF)
   (QUOTE(LAMBDA(S A)
         (PUTPROP(CAR S)
            (CONS LAMBDA (CDR S))
            FEXPR)))
   FEXPR)
```

Fig. 13. Duane Hanson: **Businessman** (1971) Polyester resin, talc, fiberglass, oil, and mixed media, 47 × 26 × 44 inches. Courtesy of the Virginia Museum.

In the light of this poem dada begins to look less like an eccentric aberration than an anticipation in the early years of the century of what would become commonplace by its end. The dada poets were prophets and seers in the old sense of those terms. They were not magicians who could predict the future but sensitive individuals who, by contemplating the obvious, were able to describe what most citizens could not see until many years later. By the same token, are not contemporary representational artists like Duane Hanson, Richard Estes, and Don Eddy, whose images seem more real than reality, telling us that we already live in a world in which the animate and the inanimate, the human and the artificial, are becoming indistinguishable, in which microbes are "programmed" and the robots have passed the Turing test (figs. 13 and 14)?

It may be that what happened in the early twentieth century is something like what happens along a geological fault. As the two masses grind against each other and adjust, they create a series of small shocks. Eventually the stored energies become so great that there is a major shock. Enormous amounts of energy are released, and the landscape is permanently changed.

Western culture has experienced a continuous series of minor shocks since the Renaissance. Sometime between 1890 and 1915 a major shock occurred. The release of its energies included new forms of science and of art but not all of its effects were benign. They included two world wars and a series of periods of reaction during which people tried to put the world together in the old way. The Nazi movement in Germany and the recent Iranian revolution were efforts in this direction, and perhaps the conservative movement in the United States is our own, more democratic and far more benign way of trying to set the clock back. The new consciousness of the twentieth century, however, is part of the deep structure of the mind, even the minds of those who would reject it.

It will not go away, and, therefore, we had better confront it directly and learn to live with it. For this task the poetry of nothing can be a useful teacher.

Fig. 14. Richard Estes: **Ansonia** (1977) Oil on canvas, 48 × 60 inches. Collection of the Whitney Museum of American Art. Gift of Frances and Sydney Lewis (Acq. no. 77.33). Courtesy of the Whitney Museum of American Art.

TEXT TYPE: *Meridien*
DISPLAY TYPE: *Serifa Series*
TYPESETTER: *Waldman Graphics, Inc., Pennsauken, NJ*
PRINTER: *Printing, Inc., Cheverly, MD*
PAPER: *Curtis Colophon text and Curtis Tuscan cover, blue*
DESIGN: *Adrianne Onderdonk Dudden*